W9-BMP-347

Also by Hugh Carpenter and Teri Sandison

Hot Wok
Hot Chicken
Hot Pasta
Hot Barbecue
Hot Vegetables
The Great Ribs Book
Fast Appetizers

Wok Fast

Hugh Carpenter
and Teri Sandison

TEN SPEED PRESS
Berkeley/Toronto

1⊜

Ten Speed Press
PO Box 7123
Berkeley, California 94707
www.tenspeed.com

Distributed in Australia by Simon and Schuster Australia, in Canada by Ten Speed Press Canada,
in New Zealand by Southern Publishers Group, in South Africa by Real Books, and in the
United Kingdom and Europe by Airlift Book Company.

Cover and text design by Beverly Wilson
Typography by Laurie Harty

Library of Congress Cataloging-in-Publication Data
Carpenter, Hugh.
  Wok fast / Hugh Carpenter and Teri Sandison.
      p. cm.
Includes index.
ISBN-10: 1-58008-383-8
ISBN-13: 978-1-58008-383-6
1. Wok cookery. I. Sandison, Teri. II. Title.
TX840.W65 C38   2002
641.7'7—dc21   2001005551

First printing, 2002
Printed in Hong Kong

6 7 8 9 10 — 08 07 06

To my Sista Debbie ~

Love julie "

To cooks everywhere

who enrich the lives of family

and friends by gathering them

around the table to share meals.

Contents

Introduction

Hugh fell in love with wok cooking by accident. A Chinese classmate from his first-year Mandarin class invited him to join a dinner group. Little did Hugh anticipate that in just a few hours, he would be ushered into the world of wok cooking, as four Chinese students stir-fried a succession of dishes at a Chinese professor's apartment. Delicious! Delicious! Delicious! And yet only inexpensive and mundane supermarket ingredients were chosen. Just a handful of shrimp, a few chicken breasts, and a tiny amount of ground beef enlivened the stir-fry vegetables. Only a wok and a battered rice pot rested on the stove. Yet the kitchen quickly filled with enticing smells, and the enthusiastic wok action equaled the animated dinner conversation as the guests crowded around the kitchen table.

We met in 1984 when Teri signed up for a culinary tour of China that Hugh was leading. Teri was on assignment as a food photographer for a magazine. Our Asian food and travel adventures together began there in China, as we feasted on all the classic dishes from every corner of the country.

We have remained fascinated with the action-packed, endlessly creative, inexpensive, and healthy cooking technique that has long been the touchstone of Chinese cuisine. It is the cooking technique that we turn to frequently for a fast work-night meal. As with us, you'll need no special cooking stove, wok ring, giant cleaver, round tree-stump cutting surface, exotic Asian produce, or staff of Chinese assistants—and certainly no Chinese language skills!

Just review the following brief sections on wok cooking and the helpful how-to photographs, and then choose a recipe. Start modestly. Stir-fry one of the vegetable recipes and serve it with broiled fish or barbecued steak. The next night, wok-sear a small amount of beef tenderloin before sliding it on top of a big dinner salad. Or roll stir-fried shrimp in charred flour tortillas, perhaps adding sliced avocado or papaya to the package. As your confidence grows, review the improvisation section and begin to add to your own chapter of wok creations.

Master the stir-fry dance. Listen to the food sizzling. Watch the color changing as each ingredient quickly becomes perfectly cooked. Smell the aromas as food caramelizes and sears against the sides of the wok. Stir and toss, then stir and toss again and again; every sense is enriched by the wok action.

You'll see that flavor-intense food is the crowning achievement of wok cooking. The high heat caramelizes the sugars in the vegetables, sears and browns meat, and evaporates marinades into flavor-intense essences. Seafood is flash-cooked so quickly that the ocean flavor is locked inside before the exterior has a chance to toughen.

Wisps of smoke drift from the metal surface, scallops sizzle dramatically, vegetables capsize in rapid action, and family and friends draw near. Enticing aromas announce the arrival of another wok creation.

Hugh Carpenter and Teri Sandison

Woks

$\mathcal{W}$oks are practical, simple, cooking vessels used in China for thousands of years to create a vast range of superb recipes. Compared to frying pans, the sloping, concave sides of a wok require less cooking oil. When given a swish, stir-fry food falls to the lower, hottest part of the wok for quick, even cooking that is difficult to duplicate in other pans. If you lack the type of wok recommended here, choose a heavy, fourteen-inch cast-iron skillet to re-create *Wok Fast* recipes rather than a poorly designed wok.

Buy the heaviest, fourteen- or sixteen-inch flat-bottom wok you can find, with one long handle and a short second handle on the opposite edge. The best are the heavy steel woks made by Calphalon (about 3½ pounds) and those available at Asian markets and many cookware shops. Other woks that work well are stainless-steel, nonstick, and copper, which are available at gourmet cookware shops. Avoid electric woks, since these never generate the high heat necessary to properly sear ingredients. In addition, avoid woks that have just two short handles (the hand that stabilizes the wok during stir-frying will likely burn) or woks with just one handle (the weight and awkward shape of the pan makes it impossible to slide the food easily out of the wok). Lastly, never buy a miniature wok. These tiny woks, measuring eight to twelve inches in diameter, do not have enough surface area to maintain proper heat, even when cooking small quantities.

Whether stir-frying on a gas or electric stove, always use a flat-bottom wok. Because a larger amount of the pan comes into contact with the gas or electric heat than in a round-bottom wok, the food cooks more quickly and tastes far superior.

Round-bottom wok

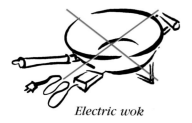

Electric wok

One handle wok

Wok with two short handles

Tiny wok

*Calphalon flat-bottom wok.
Used by the authors.*

Recommended woks

Flat-bottom steel wok with wood handles. Also recommended.

SEASONING, CLEANING, AND STORING YOUR WOK

*C*alphalon and heavy steel (sometimes called spun steel) woks require a preliminary seasoning.

Seasoning the Wok:

1. Scrub the new wok thoroughly inside and out with hot soapy water. Dry the wok completely.

3. Keep the wok in contact with the high heat. Slowly roll the oil around the sides of the wok. Use a crumpled paper towel held with tongs to make sure every part of the inside surface is coated with oil. Continue rolling the oil around the inside of the wok until it begins to smoke. The inside bottom of a steel wok will pick up a slight blue tint.

2. Place the wok over the highest heat. When the wok is hot to the touch, add ¼ cup cooking oil (peanut, safflower, or soybean oil) to the center.

4. Remove the wok from the heat. Let it cool completely, then wipe the oil from the wok. With repeated use, the seasoning gradually acquires a beautiful black nonstick luster. It is this black seasoning that contributes a special wok flavor to wok-made dishes.

Cleaning the Wok:

Provided no one scrubs the seasoning off, and the wok is only used for stir-frying, the wok *never* needs to be seasoned again. To clean the wok, place it in a sink and fill with hot water. After a few minutes, or after the meal, use hot water, a very small amount of dish soap, and a soft sponge to rub off all food particles sticking to the sides. Never scrub the wok with an abrasive pad, since this quickly strips off the seasoning.

Storing the Wok:

Dry the wok over medium heat, then store it in a dependably dry place. Do not oil the inside surface before storage, since this oil eventually turns into a rancid, sticky layer that must be scrubbed off before using the wok for the next stir-fry dish.

Vegetable Cutting Techniques

Here's the most important point:

the smaller the food is cut, the quicker it cooks, and the better it's going to taste.

*D*on't get trapped by classic Chinese wok theory! According to ancient wok wizards, everything in a dish should be cut to the same shape and size. Food prepared this way does indeed look beautiful but the practice can cause amazingly compulsive cutting techniques. We often combine different-shaped ingredients in the same dish simply to speed preparation.

Coring Bell Peppers:
Cut the ends off the pepper. Slice the pepper open and run the knife along the inside, removing the seeds and ribs.

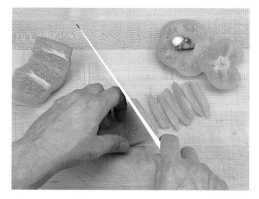

Matchstick Cutting Bell Peppers:
Cut a cored bell pepper into thin strips resembling matchsticks.

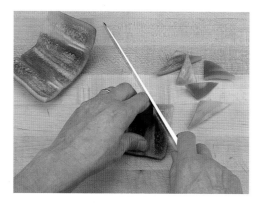

Triangle Cutting Bell Peppers:
Cut a cored bell pepper into strips. Cut one end of a strip into a triangle. Cut another end into a triangle. Repeat by cutting the pointed ends into triangles.

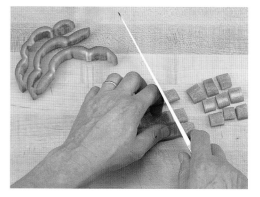

Cubing Bell Peppers:
Cut a cored bell pepper into strips. Cut across the strips to make cubes.

Roll Cutting Asparagus or Carrots:

Cut the asparagus or carrot on a sharp diagonal, then roll ¼ turn toward you and make another sharp diagonal cut. Repeat.

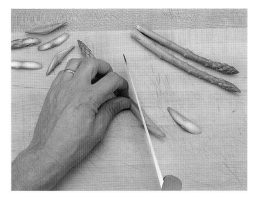

Triangle Cutting Asparagus:

Cut the asparagus on a sharp diagonal, then roll ½ turn toward you and make another diagonal cut. Repeat.

Cutting Kernels off Corncobs:

Stand cobs on end and run a knife down the cobs to remove the kernels.

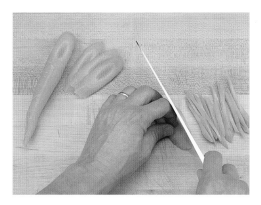

Matchstick Cutting Carrots:

Cut a large carrot on a sharp diagonal into ¼-inch-wide slices. Overlap the slices and cut into matchstick shaped pieces.

Cutting Button Mushrooms:

Cut the mushrooms through stems into slices. To cube, cut the mushrooms in half, turn 90 degrees and cut through stems into 4 wedges.

Mincing Ginger and Garlic:

Wash the ginger and trim away any wrinkled skin. Cut ginger crosswise into paper-thin slices. Mince in mini-chopper. Peel the garlic cloves. Mince in mini-chopper.

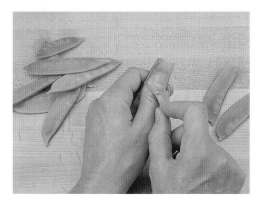

Stringing Snow Peas:

Place a thumb on the snow pea. Snap off the stem end and pull back toward your thumb, removing the fiber on both ridges.

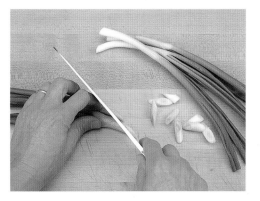

Diagonal Cutting Green Onions:

Cut the green onions on a sharp diagonal.

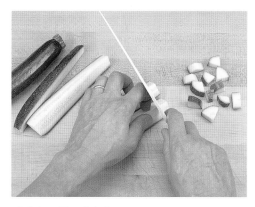

Cubing Zucchini:

Cut a zucchini in half lengthwise, then cut each half in half again lengthwise. Place the strips together and cut into cubes.

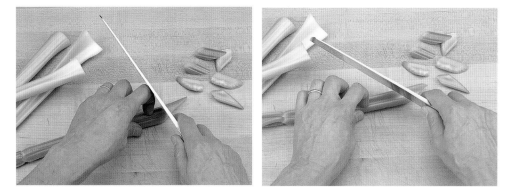 

Roll Cutting Celery and Mature Bok Choy:

Cut the celery or bok choy on a sharp diagonal. Turn the celery or bok choy over, then cut on a sharp diagonal. Return the celery or bok choy to original position and repeat cutting and rotating.

Shredding Cabbage:

Cut the stem end off the cabbage. Shred the end and cut the rest of the cabbage into shreds.

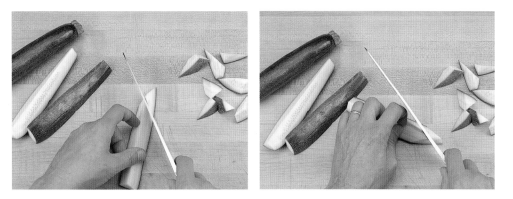 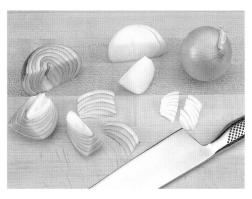

Diamond Cutting Zucchini:

Cut the zucchini into strips. Make a sharp diagonal cut across the strips. Rotate the strips about 60 degrees and cut on a diagonal. Rotate the strips back to their original position and repeat diamond cutting.

Cubing or Shredding Onion:

Cut the ends off the onion, then cut into wedges. Cut across the wedges to make cubes, or cut wedges into shreds.

From Garden to Wok

*W*e have directed you to never put more than 4 cups of vegetables in the wok unless you wish to create a vegetable soup! The exception to the rule is spinach and other leafy greens; when stir-frying such greens alone in the wok, you can add up to 8 cups.

Don't combine more than 3 vegetables for a wok dish. This minimizes preparation time, the vegetables are more likely to cook evenly, and there is less chance for the dish to become a jumble of too many different textures, colors, and tastes

Short-Cooking Vegetables: Add to the hot wok any combination of three of the following vegetables not to exceed a total of 4 cups: **thin asparagus**, **baby green beans**, **Chinese long beans**, **cabbages** (white cabbage, red cabbage, Napa cabbage, bok choy), **celery**, **Japanese eggplant**, **mushrooms** (button, cremini, shiitake, portobello, chanterelle, honey, morels but not oyster or enoki mushrooms, which become mushy when stir-fried), **onions** (yellow, red, and white onions, green onions, and chives), **peas** (garden peas, snow peas, sugar snap peas), **peppers and chiles** (all the colors of sweet peppers, as well as the entire range of spicier peppers and chiles), **summer squash** (zucchini, crookneck, patty pan, and all other squashes that become tender with just brief cooking), and **fresh water chestnuts**.

Long-Cooking Vegetables: Because of their dense texture these vegetables require longer cooking: **thick asparagus**, **broccoli**, **Brussels sprouts**, **carrots**, **cauliflower**, **potatoes**, **string beans**, and **yams**. In meat and seafood stir-fry dishes, you accelerate the cooking process by cutting the vegetables into small pieces and then briefly microwaving or blanching them in boiling water just until they brighten. Quickly chill in ice water and they can then be combined with any of the *Short-Cooking Vegetables* above, again, not to exceed a total of 4 cups. On the other hand, in vegetable-only stir-fry dishes, add the *Long-Cooking Vegetables* raw to the wok, stir-fry for a few seconds, and then add about ¼ cup liquid (water, wine, sherry, water that dried mushrooms were softened in, or chicken stock), cover the wok, and steam-cook the vegetables just until they brighten. Now add any of the *Short-Cooking Vegetables,* stir-fry these until they brighten, add a *Wok Fast* sauce, and serve at once.

Leafy Greens and Bean Sprouts, including all kinds of **lettuce**, as well as **spinach** and **bean sprouts**. If stir-frying these alone, you can add up to 8 cups. If adding these to a wok already containing meat, seafood, or other vegetables, add no more than 2 cups at the very end of the stir-fry process.

Wok Cooking

IT'S THE HEAT

Viking wok burner

*W*ok cooking and high heat are forever linked. Intense heat sears the food, locks in the moisture, flavor, and nutrition, and cooks food so quickly that meats and seafood remain tender. Vegetables taste fully cooked while still retaining a crunchy texture.

American home gas and electric stoves generate about 12,000 BTUs of heat and commercial restaurant stoves produce up to 18,000 BTUs. In comparison, Chinese restaurant stoves generate 150,000 BTUs! Because American home stoves generate so little heat, limit the wok size to fourteen to sixteen inches. Just as important, never stir-fry more than one pound of meat or seafood, or four cups of vegetables. Follow these specifications or you'll end up with wok soup!

For wok masters wanting a more intense heat, there are a number of possibilities. Several stove manufacturers, including Viking, Thermador, Dynasty, and Dynamic Cooking Systems, offer a single drop-in wok burner unit, producing approximately 30,000 BTUs of heat. These can be installed indoors or outdoors.

Crab boil burner

Chinese restaurant equipment manufacturers make a variety of freestanding, single-unit wok burners, generating between 50,000 and 150,000 BTUs. These can be modified to fit both indoor and outdoor kitchens. Brand names vary across the country, so you will have to check directly with Chinese restaurant suppliers listed in the phone books of cities with large Asian populations. In addition, some Asian markets sell portable single-unit wok stoves, which generate 50,000 BTUs and can be connected to a propane tank. These wok burners are designed only for outdoor use. We position a huge, twenty-four-inch wok on one of these burners and in just a few minutes of blazing action create a wok entrée to serve ten to fourteen people. Everyone gathers around to watch the action, perhaps helping to add food or the wok sauce. Thus, they become part of Team Wok and an exciting new outdoor sport is born!

Chinese portable wok burner

Stainless steel grilling "wok"

Giant Chinese wok

BE PREPARED!

The Boy Scout motto applies perfectly to wok cooking!

1. Cut the food into small pieces. The smaller the food is cut, the faster it cooks and the better it tastes.

2. Finish all preparation before beginning the stir-fry. You can complete the wok preparation up to 8 hours in advance of stir-frying.

3. Never cook more than 1 pound of meat or seafood or 4 cups of vegetables. Too much food = wok stew = family discord. If you want to double a recipe, enlist a cooking companion to stir-fry the second portion in another wok, imitating your every motion.

4. Place the ingredients next to the wok, and line them up in the order they will be added. Then close the cookbook, or write very brief cooking notes on a large sheet of paper that is posted next to the wok. Reading recipe directions and wok cooking are incompatible activities!

5. For every wok recipe, prepare a cornstarch mixture just before stir-frying. Mix 1 tablespoon cornstarch with 1 tablespoon water, plus ½ teaspoon cooking oil. At the very end of the cooking process, if the sauce looks watery, thicken it by stirring in a little of the cornstarch mixture. Stir-fry dishes with a watery sauce look unattractive and taste uninspired.

THE STIR-FRY DANCE

𝒩ote that the following are detailed general instructions that should be reviewed before wok cooking until they become second nature. Directions in the individual recipes may vary slightly.

Once you've completed the Be Prepared stage, you're ready for Wok Action!

1. Heat the wok over the *highest possible heat until very hot.* The wok can never be too hot. We tap the sides of the wok with our fingers to make sure it is evenly heated. Add 1 tablespoon of flavorless cooking oil (peanut, safflower, or soybean) to the center of the wok and roll the oil quickly but carefully around the bottom one-third of the wok. It's unnecessary to coat the entire surface. If the oil isn't added *quickly,* and then *quickly* rolled around the wok, the oil will begin to smoke heavily and will be in danger of bursting into flames. If the oil flames, remain calm. Cover the wok, and remove it from the heat.

2. When the oil just begins to give off a wisp of smoke, add the **meat** or **seafood**. Do this by placing the container close to the bottom of the wok, and *gently sliding* the food into the wok. Never drop the food into the wok, or the oil will splatter badly.

3. Stir-fry the meat or seafood, using a wooden spatula. While one hand holds the wok handle, the other stirs, lifts, and turns over the food. Spread the ingredients evenly across the surface in order to sear the food, wait 2 to 5 seconds, and then stir and toss the food again. Cook *until the color changes,* about 1 minute.

4. Remove the food from the wok. To do this, shake the wok vigorously in order to prevent the food from sticking to the wok. Note: when sliding food out of the wok, always tip the pan toward you. The wok is much better balanced in this position, and you will have more control sliding the food quickly and easily out of the wok and onto a platter or plates.

5. Return the wok to the highest heat, and add 1 to 2 tablespoons of cooking oil. Roll the oil around the sides of the wok.

6. When the oil is hot, add the **veg-etables**. Stir-fry the vegetables *until their color brightens,* about 1 to 2 minutes. If the vegetables appear about to scorch, but their color has not yet brightened, add ¼ cup of water, chicken or vegetable broth, Chinese rice wine, or dry sherry.

7. Immediately add the **wok sauce**, pouring it into the bottom one-third of the wok. Return the **meat** or **seafood** to the wok. Continue stir-frying until the sauce glazes all the ingredients and thickens slightly, about 1 minute.

8. If the sauce appears watery, pour in a little of the cornstarch mixture (see page 17): Hold the stir-fry spatula level. Pour about 1 teaspoon cornstarch mixture onto the spatula, and then stir this into the wok ingredients. This technique disperses the cornstarch evenly and quickly and prevents the sauce from becoming lumpy. When the sauce returns to a low boil, if it still has not thickened, then add a little more of the cornstarch mixture in the same way.

9. Slide the food onto a heated platter or dinner plates. Serve at once. People wait for the stir-fry dish; the stir-fry dish never waits for people.

*W*ok cooking is endlessly creative! Remember the childhood pastime of painting by numbers? This is its culinary equivalent, except that all the numbers can be switched around endlessly!

INITIAL PREPARATION

Meat Selection
Choose any raw meat that will be tender with only brief cooking. Cut ¼ to 1 pound of meat into small pieces, about ⅛ by ½ by 1 inches. Pick a marinade from page 26. Marinate anywhere from 5 minutes to 8 hours, according to instructions. If you plan to marinate for more than 20 minutes, cover and refrigerate.

Seafood Selection
Choose ¼ to 1 pound of raw shrimp, scallops, squid, or firm-fleshed fish such as tuna, shark, or swordfish. Shell, devein, and butterfly the shrimp, or split them in half lengthwise. If using large scallops, slice into thin disks. Clean the squid as shown on page 52. Cut fish into ⅛ by ½ by 1-inch rectangles. If preparing fish more than 20 minutes before cooking, cover and refrigerate.

Vegetable Selection
Prepare enough non-leafy vegetables to equal 4 cups. Vegetable suggestions are listed on page 15, and you can review how to cut them on pages 12 through 14. But don't include every vegetable in your refrigerator in a single wok dish! If you use just one or two vegetables, then the preparation will go much faster. If you prepare the vegetables more than 20 minutes before cooking, cover and refrigerate.

Wok Sauce Selection
Choose any wok sauce from pages 26 through 28. Combine the ingredients. If you prepare the wok sauce more than 20 minutes before cooking, cover and refrigerate.

WOK ACTION

For meat or seafood stir-frys with vegetables
Follow the pictures on pages 18 and 19.

For meat or seafood stir-frys without vegetables
Add a few cloves of minced garlic and/or 1 tablespoon of minced ginger to the meat or seafood. Begin with step 1 on page 18 and proceed through step 3. Stir-fry the meat or seafood until it changes color, add the wok sauce and stir-fry until the sauce glazes the food.

For vegetarian stir-fry dishes
Start at step 5 on page 19. Once the oil is hot, add 1 or 2 cloves of minced garlic and/or 1 tablespoon of minced ginger. Complete steps 6 through 9.

For stir-fry meat or seafood that is placed on top of stir-fry vegetables
Stir-fry the vegetables first and then transfer these to a heated platter or dinner plates. Then stir-fry the meat or seafood, and when the color changes, add the wok sauce. When the sauce glazes the food, place the meat or seafood in the center of the stir-fry vegetables and serve.

Menu Planning

What a bore it is giving Chinese dinner parties! Why should you suffer through hours of chopping, leg cramps, and a dinner that deteriorates into a kung-fu race between wok and table?

Instead, use the wok for work-night meals. Stir-fry a little beef tenderloin and slide it onto a simple salad. Wok-fast some shrimp and roll them inside hot flour tortillas. Or serve crunchy, emerald green wok asparagus as the side dish with grilled hamburgers or meat loaf.

All the recipes in this book are designed to serve two to four people. Remember, standard American home stoves and commercial ranges don't generate enough heat to cook a double portion in a wok. To double a recipe, *think teamwork!* Enlist the aid of a friend to simultaneously stir-fry the same dish in a neighboring wok, duplicating your wok dance. Give kind but firm directions, raising your voice only when necessary!

When, occasionally, wok passions rise for a dinner party, control the impulse to include more than one *Wok Fast* recipe. It's not necessary, and the logistics could cause tears. For example, begin with an appetizer of Blackened Shrimp with Tangerine Garlic Essence (page 38), served in iceberg lettuce, Bibb lettuce, or endive cups. Follow with a hearty stew and a Caesar salad. Or start the festivities with gravlax, then as the entrée match Almond Duck (page 75) with wild rice, followed by a simple salad and a triumphant rich chocolate conclusion! Or enjoy a vegetarian meal of roasted eggplant dip, Singapore Coconut Pasta (page 99), cobb salad, and fresh berries with raspberry-cabernet sauce.

Think outside the box! Don't get stuck in the Chinese rut of serving every wok dish with steamed white rice! What a bore. Break with tradition and serve *Wok Fast* dishes with wild rice, bulgur wheat, garlic bread, warm sourdough rolls, oven-roasted fingerling potatoes, couscous, or even cornbread muffins. Make polenta in the morning and spread it in a thin layer on a baking pan; then brush the polenta with butter or oil and broil until crisp (about 8 minutes); serve with a *Wok Fast* meat or seafood dish. As an alternative, hours before dinner, char some flour tortillas, then stack and wrap them in a foil packet. When you are about to embark on a *Wok Fast* dish, warm the tortillas in a 325° oven for 15 minutes. Or serve any of these stir-fry dishes on cooked American or Italian pasta, or with Asian noodles such as fresh rice noodles, udon, buckwheat soba, or somen noodles.

Go ahead! Try these ideas!

Your friends will love the simpler menu format and the innovative mix of wok food with other non-Asian courses.

Asian Condiments

The quality of Asian condiments plays a key factor in the taste of wok food. Brands differ greatly in quality, with the most mediocre brands sold by American supermarkets. The brands recommended here are widely viewed by Asian cooks as the best, and are available throughout the country in Chinese, Vietnamese, and Thai markets. Since all the Asian condiments last indefinitely at room temperature or refrigerated, buy extra to minimize shopping trips. If you are unsure where the nearest Asian market is located, just ask the owner of your favorite Asian restaurant for the closest shopping source.

Black Beans, Salted, and Black Bean Garlic Sauce: Also called fermented black beans, these are small, wrinkled, salted black beans that add an earthy, fragrant flavor to sauces. They are completely different from Latin American black beans. Salted black beans must always be rinsed and coarsely chopped, and then may be combined with ginger, garlic, and often chiles. We prefer the taste of salted black beans, rather than the more convenient black bean garlic sauce. The latter is not only less complex tasting, but is much saltier. Best Brands: Yang Jiang Preserved Beans with Ginger or Lee Kum Kee Black Bean Garlic Sauce. Substitute: None.

Chiles, Fresh: The smaller the chile, the spicier its taste. Over 80 percent of the heat is concentrated in the ribs and seeds. To use, discard the stem, and then mince the chile, with its seeds, in an electric mini-chopper, or by hand. Substitute: Asian chile sauce.

Chile Sauce, Asian: This is a general term covering many Asian chile sauces, variously labeled as chile paste, chile sauce, and chile paste with garlic. Refrigerate after opening. Best Brand: Rooster Brand Delicious Hot Chile Garlic Sauce. Substitutes: Your favorite hot sauce or fresh chiles.

Coconut Milk: Used to add flavor and body to stir-fry sauces. Always choose a Thai brand whose ingredients are just coconut and water. Stir or shake the coconut milk vigorously before using. Once opened, coconut milk is highly perishable and should be refrigerated no longer than 1 week. Best Brand: Chaokoh brand from Thailand. Note: Never substitute low-fat coconut milk, which tastes terrible!

Cooking Oil, Flavorless: Any tasteless oil that has a high smoking temperature, such as peanut, safflower, soybean, or corn oil.

Dry Sherry or Rice Wine: Always use good-quality dry sherry. For a more authentic taste, use Chinese rice wine (not to be confused with rice vinegar). Best Brands: Pagoda Brand Shao Xing Rice Wine or Pagoda Brand Shao Hsing Hua Tiao Chiew.

Fish Sauce, Thai or Vietnamese: Fish sauce, which is made by fermenting anchovies or other fish in brine, is used in Thai and Vietnamese cooking the way soy sauce is used in Chinese cooking. Always buy fish sauce produced in Thailand or Vietnam, since they have the lowest salt content. Once opened, fish sauce lasts indefinitely at room temperature. Best Brands: Three Crab Brand, Phu Quoc Flying Lion Brand, or Tiparos Brand Fish Sauce. Substitute: Thin soy sauce, although the flavor is quite different.

Ginger, Fresh: These pungent and spicy, knobby brown roots are sold by all supermarkets in the produce section. Buy firm ginger with smooth skin. It is unnecessary to peel ginger unless the skin is wrinkled. To use, wash the ginger thoroughly, then cut crosswise into paper-thin slices and mince very finely in an electric mini-chopper or with a sharp knife. Store uncut ginger in the refrigerator, at room temperature, or even inside resealable bags in the freezer. Substitute: None.

Hoisin Sauce: This thick and sweet, spicy, dark condiment is made with soy beans, chiles, garlic, ginger, and sugar. Once opened, it keeps indefinitely at room temperature. Best Brand: Koon Chun Hoisin Sauce. Substitute: None.

Oyster Sauce: Also called oyster-flavored sauce, this sauce gives a rich taste to a dish without a hint of its seafood origins. A pinch of sugar is usually added to dishes using oyster sauce, to counteract the slightly salty taste. Keeps indefinitely in the refrigerator. Best Brands: Sa Cheng Oyster Flavored Sauce; Hop Sing Lung Oyster Sauce; and Lee Kum Kee Oyster Flavored Sauce, Old Brand. Substitute: None.

Plum Sauce: This sauce is made with plums, apricots, garlic, red chiles, sugar, vinegar, salt, and water. Plum sauce is available at most supermarkets. Once opened, it lasts indefinitely in the refrigerator. Best Brand: Koon Chun Plum Sauce. Substitute: Your favorite chutney.

Rice Vinegar: Japanese rice vinegar has 4 to 5 percent acidity, as compared to American and European vinegar with 6 to 7 percent acidity, and the very mild Chinese vinegar (2½ percent). For all recipes calling for rice vinegar, use a good Japanese rice vinegar. Don't buy seasoned rice vinegar, which contains sugar and sometimes MSG. Best Brands: Marukan or Mitsukan. Substitute: None.

Sesame Oil, Dark: This is a nutty, dark golden brown oil made from toasted crushed sesame seeds. Do not confuse dark sesame oil with the clear-colored sesame oil, which has no flavor, or black sesame oil, which has far too strong a taste. Dark sesame oil is used just to add flavor to stir-fry dishes and never as a cooking oil since it smokes at a very low temperature. Dark sesame oil will last for at least a year at room temperature and indefinitely in the refrigerator. Best Brand: Kadoya Sesame Oil. Substitute: None.

Sesame Seeds, White: Buy white sesame seeds in the spice section of every American supermarket. Avoid pre-toasted sesame seeds, which are inferior in taste.

Soy Sauce, Dark: Dark, heavy, or black soy sauce is thin soy sauce with the addition of molasses or caramel, and is used to add a richer flavor and color to sauces, stews, and curries. It is indispensable in marinades for meat. Never confuse dark soy sauce with thick soy sauce sold in jars, which is a syrup-like molasses. Once opened, dark soy sauce keeps indefinitely at room temperature. Best Brand: Pearl River Bridge Brand Mushroom Soy Sauce. Substitute: Thin soy sauce.

Soy Sauce, Thin: Thin or light soy sauce is a watery, mildly salty liquid made from soy beans, roasted wheat, yeast, and salt. If you are concerned about sodium, reduce the quantity of soy sauce in a recipe, rather than using the inferior-tasting, more expensive low-sodium brands. Best Brands: Pearl River Bridge Brand Golden Label Superior Soya Sauce, Koon Chun Brand Thin Soy Sauce, or Kikkoman Regular Soy Sauce. Substitute: Equal parts dark soy sauce and water.

Szechwan Peppercorns: These are small reddish-brown seeds, all partly open, that have a beautiful aromatic flavor but are not related to black or white peppercorns. They are available at all Asian markets. To use, toast Szechwan peppercorns in a dry sauté pan over high heat until they smoke lightly. Cool, then grind in an electric spice grinder or pound in a mortar and sift the ground pepper through a medium-meshed sieve to remove the exterior brown shells. Store ground Szechwan peppercorns as you would other spices, for no longer than 6 months. Substitute: None.

Wok Marinades and Sauces

*M*arinades and wok sauces are essential for creating great-tasting stir-fry dishes. It's the marinades and sauces that add the unique flavor to wok food. Every recipe in this book refers to a particular marinade and/or sauce listed in this section. Since all these marinades and sauces can be used interchangeably, there are infinite ways to vary each and every recipe.

MARINADES

How Far Ahead to Make
Marinades that have citrus juice and/or fresh herbs must be made within 24 hours of use and kept covered and refrigerated. All other marinades will last indefinitely in the refrigerator. If you want to quicken preparation time, make your favorite marinade in a large quantity and stockpile it in the refrigerator.

What to Marinate
All meat, already cut into small pieces for stir-frying, must be marinated. Otherwise, the meat will stick to the wok and will not have a complex taste. On the other hand, shrimp, scallops, and squid are not marinated. These shellfish will steam in the marinade and the oil will splatter. Firm fish such as tuna, swordfish, yellowtail, shark, halibut, and salmon can be marinated.

How Long to Marinate
Marinate meat from 5 minutes up to 8 hours, covered and refrigerated. Remember, because the meat is cut into very small pieces, marinating longer than 30 minutes does not improve (nor does it harm) the flavor of the meat. Marinate firm fish no longer than 15 minutes.

Matching Ingredients with Marinades
All the marinades can be used interchangeably.

How Much Marinade to Mix with the Food
The ideal amount to mix with 1 pound of meat is 4 to 5 tablespoons of marinade; use 3 tablespoons of marinade for firm fish. If you use a larger amount of marinade, the food will boil in the marinade and the oil will splatter.

Using Marinades as Sauces
Instead of using a wok sauce, we often use marinades as a sauce to flavor stir-fry shrimp, scallops, tuna, or vegetables. Add the marinade during the final few seconds of stir-frying.

Varying Marinades
The flavor of marinades can be varied by adding up to 1 tablespoon each of one or more of the following: minced garlic, shallots, or ginger; grated citrus zest; and/or chopped fresh chiles, mint, cilantro, and basil.

SAUCES

How Far Ahead to Make
Same as described for marinades (see above).

Matching Ingredients with Sauces
All the sauces can be used interchangeably.

When to Add Wok Sauces
Always add the sauce during the final seconds of stir-frying. Because cornstarch can settle into a hard layer at the bottom of the sauce, always give the sauce a vigorous stir before adding it to the wok.

How to Add the Wok Sauce
Pour the sauce around the bottom one-third of the wok in a quick circular motion.

How Much Wok Sauce to Add
Most of the sauces in this book make between ½ and ¾ cup. If you prefer more sauce, it's better to increase the volume by adding ¼ to ½ cup chicken broth, vegetable broth, white wine, or water rather than doubling strong-tasting ingredients like soy sauce, oyster sauce, chile sauce, and sesame oil.

Thickening Wok Sauces
All the sauces contain a little cornstarch so that the sauce will form a beautiful glaze on the food. If no thickener is used, the sauce will form watery, unattractive puddles on the bottom of the plate. In place of the cornstarch, you can use potato starch, rice starch, tapioca starch, or arrowroot (but not flour).

How to Rescue a Watery Wok Sauce
Here's a secret tip not included in the recipe directions. Just prior to beginning the stir-fry process, *always* combine in a little container: 1 tablespoon cornstarch, 1 tablespoon cold water, and ½ teaspoon flavorless cooking oil. At the end of the stir-fry process, if the vegetables have expelled some of their moisture, thus diluting and thinning the consistency of the sauce, tighten the sauce by stirring in approximately 2 teaspoons of this prepared cornstarch mixture. If the sauce doesn't thicken nicely the moment it returns to a boil, add a little more. Incidentally, the cooking oil in the cornstarch mixture stops the sauce from lumping or acquiring a cornstarch-y taste.

All-Purpose Chinese Marinade

1 tablespoon dark soy sauce
1 tablespoon hoisin sauce
1 tablespoon dry sherry or
    Chinese rice wine
1 tablespoon dark sesame oil
Several grinds black pepper, or up to
    1 teaspoon Asian chile sauce

All-Purpose Thai Marinade

2 tablespoons Thai or Vietnamese
    fish sauce
1 tablespoon grated lime zest
1 tablespoon freshly squeezed
    lime juice
1 tablespoon honey
1 tablespoon dark sesame oil
2 fresh serrano chiles, minced
    (including seeds)
2 cloves garlic, finely minced
2 tablespoons minced cilantro sprigs

All-Purpose Fish Marinade

1 tablespoon thin soy sauce
1 tablespoon dry sherry or freshly
    squeezed lemon or lime juice
1 teaspoon dark sesame oil

Orange-Curry Marinade

1 tablespoon curry powder
1 tablespoon hoisin sauce
1 tablespoon dark sesame oil
1 tablespoon dark soy sauce or
    oyster sauce
1 tablespoon dry sherry or Chinese
    rice wine
1/2 teaspoon Asian chile sauce
2 teaspoons grated orange zest

East-West Marinade

3 tablespoons puréed olives or tapenade
2 tablespoons balsamic vinegar
1 tablespoon thin soy sauce
1 tablespoon extra virgin olive oil
1 tablespoon grated lemon zest
1/2 teaspoon crushed red pepper flakes
    or Asian chile sauce
2 cloves garlic, finely minc

Spicy Tangerine Marinade

1 tablespoon grated tangerine or
    orange zest
1 tablespoon thin soy sauce
1 tablespoon dry sherry or Chinese
    rice wine
1 tablespoon flavorless cooking oil
1 tablespoon honey
2 teaspoons Asian chile sauce

Sweet-and-Sour Lemon Sauce

1 tablespoon grated lemon zest
1 tablespoon finely minced fresh ginger
1/3 cup chicken broth
3 tablespoons freshly squeezed
    lemon juice
1 tablespoon thin soy sauce
2 tablespoons honey
2 teaspoons cornstarch
1 teaspoon Asian chile sauce

Cantonese Stir-Fry Sauce

1/4 cup chicken broth
1/4 cup dry sherry or Chinese rice wine
2 tablespoons oyster sauce
1 tablespoon dark sesame oil
2 teaspoons cornstarch
1/2 teaspoon sugar
1/2 teaspoon freshly ground black pepper

Ginger-Butter Sauce

1/4 cup finely minced fresh ginger
1/4 cup chicken broth
1/4 cup white wine
3 tablespoons melted unsalted butter
2 tablespoons oyster sauce
1 tablespoon dark sesame oil
2 teaspoons cornstarch
1 teaspoon sugar
1/2 teaspoon freshly ground black pepper

Singapore Coconut-Herb Sauce

1/2 cup unsweetened coconut milk
3 tablespoons dry sherry or Chinese
    rice wine
2 tablespoons Thai or Vietnamese
    fish sauce
1 tablespoon hoisin sauce
2 teaspoons curry powder
2 teaspoons cornstarch
1 teaspoon Asian chile sauce
1/4 cup finely chopped fresh mint
1/4 cup finely chopped fresh basil

Thai Coconut Sauce

½ cup unsweetened coconut milk
¼ cup dry sherry or Chinese rice wine
¼ cup tomato sauce
2 tablespoons oyster sauce
2 teaspoons cornstarch
1 teaspoon Asian chile sauce

Asian Garlic Sauce

6 cloves roasted mashed garlic (sold in
    the deli cases of some markets)
¼ cup chicken broth
2 tablespoons dry sherry or Chinese
    rice wine
2 tablespoons oyster sauce
2 tablespoons dark sesame oil
2 teaspoons cornstarch
1 teaspoon Asian chile sauce
½ teaspoon sugar

Essential Vegi Stir-Fry Sauce

¼ cup vegetable broth
2 tablespoons dry sherry or Chinese
    rice wine
2 tablespoons thin soy sauce
1 tablespoon dark sesame oil
2 teaspoons cornstarch
½ teaspoon sugar
¼ teaspoon freshly ground black pepper

Szechwan Hoisin-Honey Sauce

¼ cup chicken broth
¼ cup dry sherry or Chinese rice wine
2 tablespoons hoisin sauce
2 tablespoons honey
1 tablespoon dark sesame oil
2 teaspoons Asian chile sauce
2 teaspoons cornstarch

Really Risqué Sauce

¼ cup dry sherry or Chinese rice wine
¼ cup tomato sauce
3 tablespoons oyster sauce
1 tablespoon hoisin sauce
1 tablespoon dark sesame oil
2 teaspoons cornstarch
½ teaspoon freshly ground black pepper

Spicy Peanut Stir-Fry Sauce

3 tablespoons chicken broth
3 tablespoons dry sherry or Chinese
    rice wine
3 tablespoons creamy peanut butter
2 tablespoons oyster sauce
1 tablespoon hoisin sauce
1 tablespoon dark sesame oil
1 tablespoon Asian chile sauce
2 teaspoons cornstarch

Thai Black Bean Sauce

1½ cup chicken broth
2 teaspoons black bean garlic sauce, or
    1 tablespoon salted black beans,
    rinsed and finely chopped
1 tablespoon hoisin sauce
2 teaspoons grated lime zest
2 tablespoons freshly squeezed
    lime juice
2 teaspoons Asian chile sauce
2 teaspoons cornstarch
¼ cup chopped fresh basil

Spicy Tangerine Sauce

1 teaspoon grated tangerine or
    orange zest
⅓ cup freshly squeezed tangerine or
    orange juice
¼ cup dry sherry or Chinese rice wine
2 tablespoons oyster sauce
1 tablespoon hoisin sauce
1 tablespoon dark sesame oil
2 teaspoons Asian chile sauce
2 teaspoons cornstarch

Cantonese Black Bean Sauce

¼ cup chicken broth
¼ cup dry sherry or Chinese rice wine
1 tablespoon thin soy sauce
1 tablespoon dark sesame oil
2 teaspoons black bean garlic sauce, or
    1 tablespoon salted black beans,
    rinsed and finely chopped
2 teaspoons cornstarch
1 teaspoon sugar
½ teaspoon freshly ground black pepper
    or Asian chile sauce

Thai High Sauce

1 teaspoon grated lime zest
1/4 cup chicken broth
1/4 cup dry sherry or Chinese rice wine
2 tablespoons freshly squeezed lime juice
2 tablespoons hoisin sauce
2 tablespoons Thai or Vietnamese
    fish sauce
1 tablespoon dark soy sauce
2 teaspoons cornstarch
1 teaspoon Asian chile sauce
2 tablespoons finely minced fresh ginger
2 cloves garlic, finely minced
1 whole green onion, minced
2 tablespoons finely chopped cilantro
    sprigs or fresh basil

Szechwan Marinade/Sauce

2 tablespoons dry sherry or Chinese
    rice wine
1 tablespoon dark sesame oil
1 tablespoon hoisin sauce
1 tablespoon dark soy sauce
1 tablespoon honey
2 teaspoons Asian chile sauce
2 cloves garlic, finely minced
2 tablespoons finely minced fresh ginger
3 tablespoons minced green onion
2 tablespoons chopped cilantro sprigs

Hoisin Tangerine Sauce

1 teaspoon grated tangerine or
    orange zest
1/2 cup freshly squeezed tangerine or
    orange juice
3 tablespoons hoisin sauce
2 tablespoons thin soy sauce
2 teaspoons dark sesame oil
2 teaspoons cornstarch

Thai Chile-Mint-Lime Sauce

1/4 cup chicken broth
2 teaspoons grated lime zest
2 tablespoons freshly squeezed lime juice
2 tablespoons Thai or Vietnamese
    fish sauce
1 tablespoon honey
1 tablespoon Asian chile sauce
2 teaspoons cornstarch
2 tablespoons chopped fresh mint

Smoky Chipotle Chile Sauce

2 tablespoons finely minced chipotle
    chiles, including seeds
2 teaspoons grated lime zest
1/4 cup chicken broth
2 tablespoons dry sherry or Chinese
    rice wine
2 tablespoons freshly squeezed lime juice
1 tablespoon thin soy sauce
1 tablespoon brown sugar
2 teaspoons cornstarch
1/2 teaspoon ground cumin

Rosemary-Hoisin Sauce

2 tablespoons finely minced fresh
    rosemary
1/4 cup chicken broth
1/4 cup dry sherry or Chinese rice wine
2 tablespoons hoisin sauce
1 tablespoon oyster sauce
1 tablespoon thin soy sauce
2 teaspoons cornstarch
1 teaspoon Asian chile sauce

Hot and Sour Vietnamese Sauce

1/4 cup chicken broth
3 tablespoons Thai or Vietnamese
    fish sauce
2 tablespoons freshly squeezed
    lime juice
2 tablespoons light brown sugar
2 teaspoons Asian chile sauce
2 tablespoons chopped cilantro sprigs
1 tablespoon finely minced lemongrass
    (optional)
2 teaspoons cornstarch

Vegetables

*W*oks and vegetables, in their few minutes of culinary dance, achieve a perfect gastronomic marriage. The searing heat seals moisture within the vegetables, intensifies the natural sweetness by caramelizing the sugars, and fully cooks vegetables in seconds while retaining their distinctive natural textures. A subtle undercurrent of satisfying low flavor notes is added, and colors are transformed into brilliant hues. If you follow a few basic rules, and review the instructions on how to wok-cook the three major categories of vegetables on page 15, your wok vegetables will be a triumph.

Choose only the freshest vegetables— any compromise here will result in a failed dish.

Green Beans in Thai Black Bean Sauce

SERVES 2 TO 4

1 pound baby green beans or Chinese long beans, ends trimmed
3 cloves garlic, finely minced
2 tablespoons flavorless cooking oil
Thai Black Bean Sauce (page 27) or your favorite wok sauce

Advance Preparation If using very small green beans, leave them whole. If using Chinese long beans, cut them on a sharp diagonal into 2-inch lengths. Combine the beans and garlic (you will need 4 cups total). Cover and refrigerate until 5 minutes before cooking. *Can be completed to this point up to 8 hours in advance of last-minute cooking.*

Last-Minute Cooking Review the wok cooking outline on pages 18 and 19. Place a wok over high heat. When the wok is very hot, add the cooking oil. When the oil is hot, add the beans and stir-fry for 30 seconds. Pour in the sauce and immediately cover the wok. Steam the beans for 30 seconds. Remove the lid and stir. If the beans are not tender, cover the wok and cook for another 30 seconds. When tender, transfer to a platter or dinner plates and serve at once.

Dancing Peppers with Ground Lamb

SERVE 2 TO 4

5 bell peppers, various colors, stemmed and seeded
2 tablespoons flavorless cooking oil
1/4 pound ground lamb
Szechwan Marinade/Sauce (page 28) or your favorite wok sauce

Advance Preparation Cut the peppers into 1/2-inch cubes to make no more than 4 cups. Cover and refrigerate until 5 minutes before cooking. *Can be completed to this point up to 8 hours in advance of last-minute cooking.*

Last-Minute Cooking Review the wok cooking outline on pages 18 and 19. Place a wok over high heat. When the wok is very hot, add the cooking oil. When the oil is hot, add the lamb and stir and toss, pressing the meat against the sides of the wok until it is no longer pink, about 90 seconds. Add the peppers and stir-fry until brightened, about 1 minute. Pour in the sauce. Stir and toss until the sauce glazes the food, about 30 seconds. Transfer to individual bowls and serve at once.

Stir-frying a little ground meat before adding the vegetables creates a richer tasting dish. Ground lamb, pork, beef, or meat loaf mix can all be used interchangeably in any vegetable stir-fry recipe.

Wok Fast Eggplant, East-West-Style

SERVES 2 TO 4

4 to 6 Japanese or Chinese eggplants
5 cloves garlic, finely minced
2 tablespoons finely minced fresh ginger
3 tablespoons flavorless cooking oil
Rosemary-Hoisin Sauce (page 28) or your favorite wok sauce

Advance Preparation Quarter the eggplants lengthwise, then cut crosswise into 1-inch lengths. Combine the eggplants, garlic, and ginger (you will need 4 cups total). Cover and refrigerate until 5 minutes before cooking. *Can be completed to this point up to 8 hours in advance of last-minute cooking.*

Last-Minute Cooking Review the wok cooking outline on pages 18 and 19. Place a wok over high heat. When the wok is very hot, add the cooking oil. When the oil is hot, add the eggplant and stir-fry for 1 minute. Pour in the sauce and immediately cover the wok. Every 30 seconds, remove the lid and give the eggplant a brief stir before covering the wok again. If eggplant is not fully cooked but most of the sauce has boiled away, add 1/4 cup water before covering again. The eggplant is done when it darkens in color and softens slightly, about 5 minutes total cooking time. Transfer to a platter or dinner plates and serve at once.

Dancing Peppers with Ground Lamb

All the recipes in this book specify Japanese or Chinese eggplant rather than the vastly inferior globe eggplant. In addition to tasting better, Japanese and Chinese eggplants have a firmer texture, cook more quickly, absorb less oil, and don't need to be peeled. If these eggplants are sliced no thicker than 1/4 inch, they can be stir-fried in an open wok, just as sliced mushrooms and zucchini are cooked. But the finest way to appreciate the wonderful texture of Asian eggplant is to cut it into 1-inch cubes, and then combine stir-frying with steaming under the wok lid.

Zucchini in Spicy Thai Glaze

SERVES 2 TO 4

3 to 4 zucchini, patty pan, crookneck, or other summer squash
2 tablespoons finely minced fresh ginger
2 tablespoons flavorless cooking oil
Thai Chile-Mint-Lime Sauce (page 28) or your favorite wok sauce

Advance Preparation Cut the zucchini into ½-inch cubes or diamond-shaped pieces as shown on pages 13 and 14. Combine with the ginger (you will need 4 cups total). Cover and refrigerate until 5 minutes before cooking. *Can be completed to this point up to 8 hours in advance of last-minute cooking.*

Last-Minute Cooking Review the wok cooking outline on pages 18 and 19. Place a wok over high heat. When the wok is very hot, add the cooking oil. When the oil is hot, add the zucchini and stir and toss until brightened, about 1 minute. Pour in the sauce. Stir and toss until the sauce glazes the zucchini, about 30 seconds. Transfer to a platter or dinner plates and serve at once.

Mushroom Magic

SERVES 2 TO 4

1 pound firm mushrooms
2 cloves garlic, finely minced
3 tablespoons flavorless cooking oil
Cantonese Stir-Fry Sauce (page 26) or your favorite wok sauce

Advance Preparation If using shiitake mushrooms, cut off the stems. Cut the mushrooms into ⅛-inch slices. Combine the garlic and mushrooms (you will need 4 cups total). Cover and refrigerate until 5 minutes before cooking. *Can be completed to this point up to 8 hours in advance of last-minute cooking.*

Last-Minute Cooking Review the wok cooking outline on pages 18 and 19. Place a wok over high heat. When the wok is very hot, add the cooking oil. When the oil is hot, add the mushrooms and stir and toss until they just begin to wilt, 1 to 2 minutes. Pour in the sauce. Stir and toss until the sauce glazes the mushrooms, about 30 seconds. Transfer to a platter or dinner plates and serve at once.

For wok cooking, always choose firm mushrooms such as button, cremini, portobello, shiitake, chanterelles, honey, and morels. Avoid the softer oyster and enoki mushrooms, which become mushy when stir-fried.

Seared Spinach with Pine Nuts

SERVES 2 TO 4

8 cups spinach leaves, washed and dried
2 cloves garlic, finely minced
¼ cup pine nuts
East-West Marinade (page 26) or your favorite wok marinade
2 tablespoons flavorless cooking oil

Advance Preparation Preheat the oven to 325°. Combine the spinach and garlic. Cover and refrigerate until 5 minutes before cooking. Spread the pine nuts on a baking sheet and toast until golden, about 8 minutes. *Can be completed to this point up to 8 hours in advance of last-minute cooking.*

Last-Minute Cooking Review the wok cooking outline on pages 18 and 19. Place the spinach in a large bowl and add the marinade. Toss until the leaves are evenly coated with the marinade. Place a wok over high heat. When the wok is very hot, add the cooking oil. When the oil is hot, add the spinach and stir and toss until about three-quarters of the leaves are wilted, about 30 seconds. Immediately transfer to a platter or dinner plates. Sprinkle the pine nuts over and serve at once.

Crunchy Bean Sprout Stir-Fry

SERVES 2 TO 4

1 fresh red chile, or ¼ red bell pepper (optional), stemmed and seeded
1 tablespoon thin soy sauce
1 tablespoon dark sesame oil
1 teaspoon Asian chile sauce
2 cloves garlic, finely minced
2 tablespoons white sesame seeds
4 cups bean sprouts
2 tablespoons flavorless cooking oil

Advance Preparation Shred the chile. Combine the soy sauce, sesame oil, chile sauce, and garlic. Place the sesame seeds in a dry frying pan and toast until golden, about 2 minutes. Cover and refrigerate all ingredients except the sesame seeds until 5 minutes before cooking. *Can be completed to this point up to 8 hours in advance of last-minute cooking.*

Last-Minute Cooking Review the wok cooking outline on pages 18 and 19. In a large bowl, combine the bean sprouts with the chile and the soy sauce mixture. Toss until evenly coated. Place a wok over high heat. When the wok is very hot, add the cooking oil. When oil is hot, add the bean sprouts and stir and toss until just heated through, about 20 seconds. Sprinkle on the sesame seeds. Transfer to a platter or dinner plates and serve at once.

*Spinach and other leafy greens are cooked in a blazing hot wok—fast, fast, fast! Since spinach wilts and becomes a watery mess very quickly at such a high heat, the leaves are tossed with a dressing **before** entering the pan. Then, after a few seconds of stir-frying when some of the spinach leaves have still not wilted, the spinach is slid onto a platter or dinner plates. To vary the taste, substitute your favorite oil and vinegar salad dressing or any wok marinade.*

Chiles San Miguel-Style

SERVES 2 TO 4

4 pasilla or poblano chiles, stemmed and seeded
3 yellow onions
4 cloves garlic, finely minced
2 tablespoons flavorless cooking oil
1/4 cup spicy Mexican salsa or All-Purpose Chinese Marinade (page 26)

Advance Preparation Cut the chiles into 1/2-inch cubes or small rectangular pieces. Peel and cut the onions into thin segments. Combine the chiles, onions, and garlic (you will need 4 cups total). Cover and refrigerate until 5 minutes before cooking. *Can be completed to this point up to 8 hours in advance of last-minute cooking.*

Last-Minute Cooking Review the wok cooking outline on pages 18 and 19. Place a wok over high heat. When the wok is very hot, add the cooking oil. When the oil is hot, add the vegetable mixture and stir and toss until the onions separate into individual segments and the chiles brighten, about 2 minutes. Pour in the salsa. Stir and toss until the salsa glazes the food, about 30 seconds. Transfer to a platter or dinner plates and serve at once.

Whenever we visit the historic Mexican colonial town of San Miguel de Allende, we look forward to seasoning barbecued steak with spoonfuls of a spicy mix of pasilla chiles and onions, called "rajas." You can vary the choice of chiles or sweet bell peppers, choose your favorite store-bought salsa to season the stir-fry, or add a new twist by substituting one of the Asian marinades from page 26. Experiment!

Baby Bok Choy in Spicy Garlic Sauce

SERVES 2 TO 4

6 baby bok choy, or 8 stalks large bok choy
2 tablespoons flavorless cooking oil
Asian Garlic Sauce (page 27) or your favorite wok sauce

Advance Preparation If using baby bok choy, cut the bottoms off and separate the stems. Wash and pat or spin dry. If using large bok choy, roll-cut as shown on page 14. Cover and refrigerate until 5 minutes before cooking. *Can be completed to this point up to 8 hours in advance of last-minute cooking.*

Last-Minute Cooking Review the wok cooking outline on pages 18 and 19. Place a wok over high heat. When the wok is very hot, add the cooking oil. When the oil is hot, add the bok choy and stir and toss until the leaves just begin to wilt, about 30 seconds. Pour in the sauce. Stir and toss until the sauce glazes the food, about 15 seconds. Transfer to a platter or dinner plates and serve at once.

Baby bok choy, about 4 inches long, is being sold in an increasing number of markets. It's simple to prepare: you only need to cut off the bottom and then separate the leafy stems. Give these a wash and then dry in a lettuce spinner. Or you can substitute large bok choy, or any type of cabbage cut into shreds.

Chiles San Miguel–Style

Broccolini Asparation

SERVES 2 TO 4

3 bunches broccolini, about ½ pound total
2 tablespoons flavorless cooking oil
2 cloves garlic, finely minced
Essential Vegi Stir-Fry Sauce (page 27) or your favorite wok sauce

Advance Preparation Cut the broccolini on a sharp diagonal into 1½-inch lengths (you will need 4 cups total). Cover and refrigerate until 5 minutes before cooking. *Can be completed to this point up to 8 hours in advance of last-minute cooking.*

Last-Minute Cooking Review the wok cooking outline on pages 18 and 19. Place a wok over high heat. When the wok is very hot, add the cooking oil and the garlic. When the garlic begins to sizzle, but not brown, add the broccolini. Stir and toss until the broccolini brightens, about 2 minutes. Pour in the sauce. Stir and toss until the sauce glazes the food, about 30 seconds. Transfer to a platter or dinner plates and serve at once.

Broccolini is a cross between American and Chinese broccoli. Because broccolini has slender, non-fibrous stems, the entire vegetable can be cut into bite-sized pieces before being stir-fried. Some markets sell broccolini labeled as "asparation," leading to the mistaken belief among some cooks that broccolini is a cross between broccoli and asparagus.

Baby Carrots with Thai Coconut Glaze

SERVES 2 TO 4

3 bunches baby carrots, or 5 medium carrots, peeled
2 cloves garlic, finely minced
Thai Coconut Sauce (page 27) or your favorite wok sauce
2 tablespoons chopped fresh mint
2 tablespoons flavorless cooking oil

Advance Preparation If using baby carrots, trim off the ends and leave whole. If using medium carrots, roll-cut as shown on page 13. Combine the carrots and garlic (you will need 4 cups total). Combine the sauce and mint. Cover and refrigerate all ingredients until 5 minutes before cooking. *Can be completed to this point up to 8 hours in advance of last-minute cooking.*

Last-Minute Cooking Review the wok cooking outline on pages 18 and 19. Place a wok over high heat. When the wok is very hot, add the cooking oil. When the oil is hot, add the carrots and stir-fry for 30 seconds. Pour in the sauce and immediately cover the wok. Every 30 seconds, remove the lid and give the carrots a brief stir. Cover the wok and repeat the process. When the carrots brighten and are tender, about 90 seconds, remove the lid. Transfer to a platter or dinner plates and serve at once.

Except for matchstick-cut carrots, which will cook in seconds in an uncovered wok, most carrots are cut into larger pieces and need a combination of cooking techniques. This involves a preliminary stir-fry, followed by covering and steaming. To create the steam, add any of the wok sauces from this book. Or if you desire a simpler flavor, add ¼ cup of any of the following: water, white wine, vegetable broth, or chicken broth. Ideally, when the liquid boils away, the carrots will be brightly colored and fully cooked. If you've used a neutral-flavored liquid such as water or wine, season the carrots with salt and pepper or a dash of thin soy sauce and a few drops of dark sesame oil at the very end of the stir-fry process.

Cauliflower in Lemon Essence

SERVES 2 TO 4

1 medium head cauliflower
2 tablespoons finely minced fresh ginger
2 tablespoons flavorless cooking oil
Sweet-and-Sour Lemon Sauce (page 26) or your favorite wok sauce

Advance Preparation Using a paring knife, cut away the center stem of the cauliflower. Separate into individual florets. Combine the cauliflower and ginger (you will need 4 cups total). Cover and refrigerate until 5 minutes before cooking. *Can be completed to this point up to 8 hours in advance of last-minute cooking.*

Last-Minute Cooking Review the wok cooking outline on pages 18 and 19. Place a wok over high heat. When the wok is very hot, add the cooking oil. When the oil is hot, add the cauliflower and stir-fry for 30 seconds. Pour in the sauce and immediately cover the wok. Every 30 seconds, remove the lid and briefly stir the cauliflower. Cover the wok and repeat the process. When the cauliflower is tender, about 2 minutes, remove the lid. Transfer to a platter or dinner plates and serve at once.

Grating Citrus:
Grate the citrus skin on a microplane or rasp.

Asparagus in Ginger-Butter Sauce

SERVES 2 TO 4

1 pound asparagus, woody ends snapped off
2 tablespoons flavorless cooking oil
Ginger-Butter Sauce (page 26) or your favorite wok sauce

Advance Preparation Cut thin asparagus diagonally into 1-inch lengths, or roll-cut thicker asparagus as shown on page 13 (you will need 4 cups total). Cover and refrigerate until 5 minutes before cooking. *Can be completed to this point up to 8 hours in advance of last-minute cooking.*

Last-Minute Cooking Review the wok cooking outline on pages 18 and 19. Place a wok over high heat. When the wok is very hot, add the cooking oil. When the oil is hot, add the asparagus and stir and toss until brightened, about 2 minutes. Pour in the sauce. Stir and toss until the sauce glazes the asparagus, about 30 seconds. Transfer to a platter or dinner plates and serve at once.

Few vegetables are as well-loved as asparagus. Wok cooking intensifies asparagus's flavor while maintaining its crunchy texture. To extend the freshness of asparagus, trim the ends by 1 inch, stand in 3 inches of cold water, cover with a plastic bag, and refrigerate.

Shrimp

*W*ok-seared shrimp are a great taste and texture sensation, whose triumphs far outweigh the tedium of shelling and deveining. We always choose large raw shrimp in order to speed the preparation along, but any size shrimp can be substituted. We also prefer the freshwater shrimp, often called "black tiger prawns" that are most frequently from Thailand, numbering 16 per pound. These have a pure shrimp flavor, while ocean shrimp can have a distinct, metallic preservative taste that is ruinous to any dish. Most of the following recipes specify splitting the shrimp in half lengthwise along the vein. But large shrimp look beautiful cut crosswise in ¼-inch "rounds," or you can cut the whole shrimp into thin pieces on a sharp diagonal. You'll notice that all shrimp recipes and most other wok seafood recipes don't use marinating as a technique. When marinated shrimp are added to the wok, they will steam in their marinade and the stir-fry oil can splatter badly.

*I*f you stir-fry shrimp in their shells, they will be more tender and the flavor of the shells will contribute a more intense "shrimp" taste. However, if you don't want messy hands while eating, shell the shrimp in advance of cooking and cut them deeply along the top so they are nearly split in half.

Blackened Shrimp with Tangerine Garlic Essence

SERVES 2 TO 4

1 pound large raw shrimp, shells on
2 tablespoons flavorless cooking oil
3 cloves garlic, finely minced
Spicy Tangerine Marinade (page 26) or your favorite wok sauce

Advance Preparation Using scissors or a thin knife, cut along the top of the shrimp shell to expose the vein. Rinse out the vein, being careful to keep the shell intact. Cover and refrigerate until 5 minutes before cooking. Combine the cooking oil and garlic. *Can be completed to this point up to 8 hours in advance of last-minute cooking.*

Last-Minute Cooking Review the wok cooking outline on pages 18 and 19. Place a wok over high heat. When the wok is very hot, add the oil-garlic mixture and sauté for a few seconds. Add the shrimp and stir and toss until the shells turn pink (a few black scorch marks are fine), about 90 seconds. Cut one in half; it should be white in the center. During the last 30 seconds of cooking, add the marinade and stir until it thickens. Transfer to a platter or plates and serve hot, at room temperature, or cold. Each person peels off the shells at the table.

Vietnamese Hot and Sour Shrimp

SERVES 2 TO 4

1 pound large shrimp, shelled and deveined
1 pound thin asparagus, woody ends snapped off
2 cloves garlic, finely minced
2 tablespoons finely minced fresh ginger
¼ cup pine nuts
Hot and Sour Vietnamese Sauce (page 28) or your favorite wok sauce
3 tablespoons flavorless cooking oil

Advance Preparation Preheat the oven to 325°. Cut the shrimp in half lengthwise. Cut the asparagus on a sharp diagonal into 1-inch lengths. Combine the asparagus, garlic, and ginger (you will need 4 cups total). Spread the pine nuts on a baking sheet and toast until golden, about 8 minutes. Remove the nuts from the oven and crush lightly with a rolling pin. Cover and refrigerate all ingredients except the pine nuts until 5 minutes before cooking. *Can be completed to this point up to 8 hours in advance of last-minute cooking.*

Last-Minute Cooking Review the wok cooking outline on pages 18 and 19. Place a wok over high heat. When the wok is very hot, add 1½ tablespoons of the oil. When the oil is hot, add the shrimp and stir-fry until they turn slightly pink, about 1 minute. Transfer to a plate and return the wok to high heat. Add the remaining 1½ tablespoons oil. When it is hot, add the asparagus mixture and stir-fry until brightened, about 1 minute. Pour in the sauce and return the shrimp to the wok. Stir and toss until the sauce glazes the food, about 30 seconds. Transfer to a platter or dinner plates, sprinkle the crushed pine nuts over, and serve at once.

We relished a stir-fry shrimp dish similar to this at a tiny restaurant in Saigon, now Ho Chi Minh City. If you want to add a more complex taste, add 2 tablespoons finely minced lemongrass leaves to the sauce. Store-bought lemongrass won't work here because it's the very fresh, long green leaves, rather than the stalk, that are used for their alluring, subtle flavor. If you live in a frost-free area, stick a stalk of store-bought lemongrass in potting soil, and it will soon root itself and grow into a thick clump.

Wok-Seared Pesto Shrimp

SERVES 2 TO 4

1 pound large raw shrimp, shelled and deveined
2 tablespoons flavorless cooking oil
2 cups cherry tomatoes, quartered
½ cup store-bought or homemade pesto sauce
1 teaspoon Asian chile sauce (optional)
½ lemon

Advance Preparation Cut the shrimp in half lengthwise. Cover and refrigerate until 5 minutes before cooking. *Can be completed to this point up to 8 hours in advance of last-minute cooking.*

Last-Minute Cooking Review the wok cooking outline on pages 18 and 19. Place a wok over high heat. When the wok is very hot, add the oil. When the oil is hot, add the shrimp and stir-fry until they turn slightly pink, about 1 minute. Add the tomatoes and pesto sauce. Stir and toss until the sauce glazes the shrimp, about 30 seconds. Stir in the chile sauce. Transfer to a platter or dinner plates. Squeeze a little lemon juice over the top and serve at once.

Lemon Shrimp

SERVES 2 TO 4

1 pound large raw shrimp, shelled and deveined
¼ cup pine nuts
2 tablespoons flavorless cooking oil
Sweet-and-Sour Lemon Sauce (page 26) or your favorite wok sauce
¼ cup chopped cilantro sprigs

Advance Preparation Preheat the oven to 325°. Butterfly the shrimp as shown here. Cover and refrigerate until 5 minutes before cooking. Spread the pine nuts on a baking sheet and toast until golden, about 8 minutes. *Can be completed to this point up to 8 hours in advance of last-minute cooking.*

Last-Minute Cooking Review the wok cooking outline on pages 18 and 19. Place a wok over high heat. When the wok is very hot, add the oil. When the oil is hot, add the shrimp and stir-fry until they turn slightly pink, about 2 minutes. Pour in the sauce and stir and toss until the sauce glazes the food, about 30 seconds. Stir in the cilantro and pine nuts. Transfer to a platter or dinner plates and serve at once.

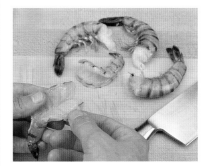

Butterflying Shrimp:
Shell the shrimp. Cut deeply along top of each shrimp and remove the vein if present.

Shrimp in Classic Cantonese Black Bean Sauce

SERVES 2 TO 4

1 pound large raw shrimp, shelled and deveined
3 medium zucchini
1 red onion
2 tablespoons finely minced fresh ginger
3 tablespoons flavorless cooking oil
Cantonese Black Bean Sauce (page 27) or your favorite wok sauce

Advance Preparation Cut the shrimp in half lengthwise. Cut the zucchini into cubes as shown on page 13. Peel and cut the red onion into 1-inch cubes. Combine the zucchini, onion, and ginger (you will need 4 cups total). Cover and refrigerate all ingredients until 5 minutes before cooking. *Can be completed to this point up to 8 hours in advance of last-minute cooking.*

Last-Minute Cooking Review the wok cooking outline on pages 18 and 19. Place a wok over high heat. When the wok is very hot, add 1½ tablespoons of the oil. When the oil is hot, add the shrimp and stir-fry until they turn slightly pink, about 1 minute. Transfer to a plate and return the wok to high heat. Add the remaining 1½ tablespoons oil. When it is hot, add the vegetable mixture and stir-fry until the onion separates into individual layers and the zucchini brightens, about 2 minutes. Pour in the sauce and return the shrimp to the wok. Stir and toss until the sauce glazes the food, about 30 seconds. Transfer to a platter or dinner plates and serve at once.

Lemon Shrimp

Marco Polo Shrimp

SERVES 2 TO 4

1 pound large raw shrimp, shelled and deveined
3 cloves garlic, finely minced
1 cup imported black olives, pitted
1/3 cup pine nuts
1/3 cup chicken broth
2 teaspoons cornstarch
1/2 teaspoon salt
1/2 teaspoon sugar
1/2 teaspoon crushed red pepper flakes or Asian chile sauce
1/3 cup fresh basil leaves
2 tablespoons olive oil
1/2 lemon

The saltiness of imported olives varies greatly. If the olives seem sufficiently salty, omit the salt in the chicken broth mixture, and then, if necessary, add salt to taste at the very end of the cooking process.

Advance Preparation Preheat the oven to 325°. Cut the shrimp crosswise into 1/4-inch slices and combine with the garlic. Cut the olives in half lengthwise. Spread the pine nuts on a baking sheet and toast until golden, about 8 minutes. In a small bowl, combine the chicken broth, cornstarch, salt, sugar, and pepper flakes. Cover and refrigerate all ingredients except the pine nuts until 5 minutes before cooking. *Can be completed to this point up to 8 hours in advance of last-minute cooking.*

Last-Minute Cooking Chop the basil. Review the wok cooking outline on pages 18 and 19. Place a wok over high heat. When the wok is very hot, add the oil. When the oil is hot, add the shrimp and stir-fry until they turn slightly pink, about 1 minute. Add the olives, pine nuts, basil, and chicken broth mixture. Stir and toss until the shrimp are cooked through to the center, about 30 seconds. Transfer to a platter or dinner plates. Squeeze a little lemon juice over the top and serve at once.

Shrimp in Smoky Chipotle Chile Sauce

SERVES 2 TO 4

1 pound large raw shrimp, shelled and deveined
3 cloves garlic, finely minced
2 tablespoons flavorless cooking oil
Smoky Chipotle Chile Sauce (page 28) or your favorite wok sauce
1/3 cup chopped cilantro sprigs
3 ounces soft goat cheese, crumbled

Other cuisines are easily adapted to the wok, as you can see in the following three recipes. The shrimp in chipotle sauce can also be served with grilled polenta triangles and accompanied by a watercress-pecan salad.

Advance Preparation Cut the shrimp in half lengthwise and combine with the garlic. Cover and refrigerate until 5 minutes before cooking. *Can be completed to this point up to 8 hours in advance of last-minute cooking.*

Last-Minute Cooking Review the wok cooking outline on pages 18 and 19. Place a wok over high heat. When the wok is very hot, add the oil. When the oil is hot, add the shrimp and stir-fry until they turn slightly pink, about 1 minute. Pour in the sauce. Stir and toss until the sauce glazes the shrimp, about 30 seconds. Stir in the cilantro and transfer to a platter or dinner plates. Sprinkle the goat cheese over and serve at once.

Shrimp in Smoky Chipotle Chile Sauce

Bangkok Shrimp with Button Mushrooms

If you can't find Chinese long beans, substitute the tiny green beans called haricots vert, trimmed asparagus, or zucchini cut into matchstick pieces in any recipe calling for long beans.

SERVES 2 TO 4

1 pound large raw shrimp, shelled and deveined
½ pound button mushrooms
3 ears fresh white corn, husked
3 whole green onions
2 cloves garlic, finely minced
1 tablespoon finely minced fresh ginger
Thai Coconut Sauce (page 27) or your favorite wok sauce
¼ cup chopped cilantro
3 tablespoons flavorless cooking oil

Advance Preparation Cut the shrimp crosswise into ¼-inch rounds. Cut the mushrooms into quarters. Cut the kernels from the corn cobs. Cut the green onions on a sharp diagonal into 1-inch lengths. Combine the mushrooms, garlic, and ginger; combine the corn and green onions (you will need 4 cups total). Combine the sauce and cilantro. Cover and refrigerate all ingredients until 5 minutes before cooking. *Can be completed to this point up to 8 hours in advance of last-minute cooking.*

Last-Minute Cooking Review the wok cooking outline on pages 18 and 19. Place a wok over high heat. When the wok is very hot, add 1½ tablespoons of the oil. When the oil is hot, add the shrimp and stir-fry until they turn slightly pink, about 1 minute. Transfer to a plate and return the wok to high heat. Add the remaining 1½ tablespoons oil. When it is hot, add the mushroom mixture and stir-fry until the mushrooms begin to soften, about 1 minute. Add the corn and green onions and stir-fry for 30 seconds. Pour in the sauce and return the shrimp to the wok. Stir and toss until the sauce glazes the food, about 30 seconds. Transfer to a platter or dinner plates and serve at once.

Szechwan Shrimp

SERVES 2 TO 4

1 pound large raw shrimp, shelled and deveined
2 tablespoons flavorless cooking oil
Szechwan Marinade/Sauce (page 28) or your favorite wok sauce
2 cups bean sprouts

Advance Preparation Cut the shrimp in half lengthwise. Cover and refrigerate until 5 minutes before cooking. *Can be completed to this point up to 8 hours in advance of last-minute cooking.*

Last-Minute Cooking Review the wok cooking outline on pages 18 and 19. Place a wok over high heat. When the wok is very hot, add the oil. When the oil is hot, add the shrimp and stir-fry until they turn slightly pink, about 1 minute. Add the sauce, and stir and toss until the sauce glazes the shrimp, about 30 seconds. Stir in the bean sprouts. Transfer to a platter or dinner plates and serve at once.

Bangkok Shrimp with Button Mushrooms

Scallops

*Stir-frying locks in the moisture of scallops, concentrates their intense sweetness, and preserves their extraordinary tenderness. The key for great wok scallop dishes is to purchase only **fresh** scallops. Scallops, no matter how quickly frozen or carefully thawed, immediately release their internal liquid into the wok. The sweetness disappears and the scallops toughen as they boil in their own essence. Inspect the scallops before purchasing. Fresh scallops have a pleasant odor. Thawed scallops have no odor until they begin to spoil! Fresh scallops have no surrounding liquid. Thawed scallops rest in a skim-milk-colored watery mess. There are pros and cons of "bay" versus the larger "sea" scallops: bay scallops require no preparation and are inexpensive. More expensive sea scallops need the little secondary muscle pulled away from the edge and do take more time to prepare since they have to be sliced, crosswise, into slender disks. But for intense, sweet scallop taste, sea scallops are the overwhelming winners! However, you may use bay and sliced sea scallops interchangeably in all wok recipes.*

Fire Wok Scallops with Mexican Salsa

SERVES 2 TO 4

1 pound fresh bay scallops
2 tablespoons flavorless cooking oil
1 cup homemade or store-bought salsa

Advance Preparation If the scallops are wet, pat them dry with paper towels. Cover and refrigerate until 5 minutes before cooking. *Can be completed to this point up to 8 hours in advance of last-minute cooking.*

Last-Minute Cooking Review the wok cooking outline on pages 18 and 19. Place a wok over high heat. When the wok is very hot, add the cooking oil. When the oil is hot, add the scallops and stir-fry until they firm slightly and begin to turn white, about 1 minute. Pour in the salsa and stir and toss until the salsa is piping hot and glazes the scallops, about 30 seconds. Transfer to a platter or dinner plates and serve at once.

We have had very good success using store-bought salsas made by local manufacturers, which have neither sugar nor artificial flavors added, and don't have the strange, processed taste that typifies the mass-produced salsas. If you choose a tropical fruit salsa, add it just before transferring the scallops to the plate so that the heat does not discolor the fruits.

Scallops Singapore-Style

SERVES 2 TO 4

1 pound fresh bay scallops
½ pound thin asparagus, woody ends snapped off
3 whole green onions
2 tablespoons finely minced fresh ginger
3 tablespoons flavorless cooking oil
Singapore Coconut-Herb Sauce (page 26) or your favorite wok sauce

Advance Preparation If the scallops are wet, pat them dry with paper towels. Cut the asparagus on a sharp diagonal into 1-inch pieces. Cut the green onions on a diagonal into 1-inch pieces. Combine the asparagus, onions, and ginger (you will need 4 cups total). Cover and refrigerate all ingredients until 5 minutes before cooking. *Can be completed to this point up to 8 hours in advance of last-minute cooking.*

Last-Minute Cooking Review the wok cooking outline on pages 18 and 19. Place a wok over high heat. When the wok is very hot, add 1½ tablespoons of the cooking oil. When the oil is hot, add the scallops and stir-fry until they firm slightly and begin to turn white, about 1 minute. Transfer to a plate and return the wok to high heat. Add the remaining 1½ tablespoons oil. When it is hot, add the vegetable mixture and stir-fry until brightened, about 1 minute. Pour in the sauce and return the scallops to the wok. Stir and toss until the sauce glazes the food, about 30 seconds. Transfer to a platter or dinner plates and serve at once.

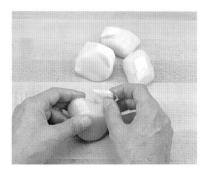

Removing the Secondary Muscle from Scallops:
Pull away the small muscle from the side of large scallops

Black Bean Thai Scallops

SERVES 2 TO 4

1 pound fresh bay scallops
3 ears white corn, husked
2 whole green onions
3 tablespoons finely minced fresh ginger
Thai Black Bean Sauce (page 27) or your favorite wok sauce
2 tablespoons chopped fresh basil
2 tablespoons flavorless cooking oil

Advance Preparation If the scallops are wet, pat them dry with paper towels. Cut the kernels from the corncobs. Cut the green onions on a sharp diagonal into ½-inch pieces, then combine with the corn and ginger. Combine the sauce and basil. Cover and refrigerate all ingredients until 5 minutes before cooking. *Can be completed to this point up to 8 hours in advance of last-minute cooking.*

Last-Minute Cooking Review the wok cooking outline on pages 18 and 19. Place a wok over high heat. When the wok is very hot, add the cooking oil. When the oil is hot, add the corn mixture and stir-fry until the green onions brighten, about 30 seconds. Add the scallops and stir-fry until they firm slightly and begin to turn white, about 1 minute. Pour in the sauce. Stir and toss until the sauce glazes the food, about 30 seconds. Transfer to a platter or dinner plates and serve at once.

Ginger Scallops with Snow Peas and Mushrooms

SERVES 2 TO 4

1 pound fresh bay scallops
2 cups small snow peas
¼ pound small button mushrooms
3 tablespoons flavorless cooking oil
Ginger-Butter Sauce (page 26) or your favorite wok sauce

Advance Preparation If the scallops are wet, pat them dry with paper towels. Snap the stem ends off the snow peas, pulling away the fiber that runs along the ridge. Cut the mushrooms into quarters. Combine the snow peas and mushrooms (you will need 4 cups total). Cover and refrigerate all ingredients until 5 minutes before cooking. *Can be completed to this point up to 8 hours in advance of last-minute cooking.*

Last-Minute Cooking Review the wok cooking outline on pages 18 and 19. Place a wok over high heat. When the wok is very hot, add 1½ tablespoons of the cooking oil. When the oil is hot, add the scallops and stir-fry until they firm slightly and begin to turn white, about 1 minute. Transfer to a plate and return the wok to high heat. Add the remaining 1½ tablespoons oil. When it is hot, add the vegetable mixture and stir-fry until brightened, about 1 minute. Pour in the sauce and return the scallops to the wok. Stir and toss until the sauce glazes the food, about 30 seconds. Transfer to a platter or dinner plates and serve at once.

Thai High Sea Scallops

SERVES 2 TO 4

1 pound fresh sea scallops
1 tablespoon flavorless cooking oil
Thai High Sauce (page 28) or your favorite wok sauce

Advance Preparation If the scallops are wet, pat them dry with paper towels. If they have a little secondary muscle along one edge, pull this off and discard as shown on page 47. Stand scallops on their edge and cut each crosswise into 3 to 4 slices. Cover and refrigerate until 5 minutes before cooking. *Can be completed to this point up to 8 hours in advance of last-minute cooking.*

Last-Minute Cooking Review the wok cooking outline on pages 18 and 19. Place a wok over high heat. When the wok is very hot, add the cooking oil. When the oil is hot, add the scallops and stir-fry until they firm slightly and begin to turn white, about 1 minute. Pour in the sauce. Stir and toss until the sauce glazes the scallops, about 30 seconds. Transfer to a platter or dinner plates and serve at once.

Ginger Scallops with Snow Peas and Mushrooms

Squid

*W*hile squid is a tremendously popular choice at Asian and Italian restaurants, few home cooks duplicate these dishes because of the rather messy and time-consuming cleaning process. Happily, some markets are now selling cleaned squid. But even if you must perform this task yourself, the taste results are worth the time. Try substituting squid for any of the seafood recipes in this book. Just remember, the best way to pre-cook squid is not to use a wok! We stir the squid into rapidly boiling water, cook it for 10 seconds, drain well, and then transfer it to a very hot wok. The preliminary blanching locks all the sweet moisture into the squid before it is glazed with the stir-fry vegetables and sauce.

Flower Blossom Squid

SERVES 2 TO 4

1 pound small squid, fresh or frozen and thawed
6 heads baby bok choy
Ginger-Butter Sauce (page 26) or your favorite wok sauce
¼ cup chopped fresh mint
2 tablespoons flavorless cooking oil

Advance Preparation If necessary, clean the squid as shown on page 52. Cut the ends off the baby bok choy and separate the leaves so that you have no more than 4 cups. Combine the sauce and the mint. Cover and refrigerate all ingredients until 5 minutes before cooking. *Can be completed to this point up to 8 hours in advance of last-minute cooking.*

Last-Minute Cooking Review the wok cooking outline on pages 18 and 19. Bring 4 quarts of water to a rapid boil in a large pot. Place a colander in the sink. Place a wok over high heat. When the wok is very hot, stir the squid into the boiling water. As soon as the squid turns white, about 5 seconds, dump it into the colander and shake dry. Add the cooking oil to the hot wok. When the oil is hot, add the bok choy. Stir-fry until the greens brighten, about 1 minute. Add the squid and the sauce. Stir and toss until the sauce glazes the food, about 1 minute. Transfer to a platter or dinner plates and serve at once.

Flower Blossom Squid

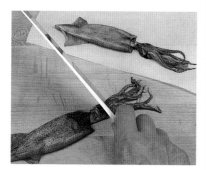

Cleaning Squid:

Pull away the squid tentacles. Cut the tentacles off just above the eyes. Pull away the mouth or beak and discard.

Under cold running water, rub off the outside membrane/skin.

Cut open the body and rinse the inside, then cut into bite-sized pieces. Or, squeeze the squid tube, pushing out the inside organs, pull out the quill; then cut across the body to make small circles.

Sweet, Spicy, Sour Squid

SERVES 2 TO 4

1 pound small squid, fresh or frozen and thawed
1 tablespoon flavorless cooking oil
3 cloves garlic, finely minced
Thai Chile-Mint-Lime Sauce (page 28) or your favorite wok sauce

Advance Preparation If necessary, clean the squid as shown here, then cut into bite-sized pieces. Cover and refrigerate until 5 minutes before cooking. *Can be completed to this point up to 8 hours in advance of last-minute cooking.*

Last-Minute Cooking Review the wok cooking outline on pages 18 and 19. Bring 4 quarts of water to a rapid boil in a large pot. Place a colander in the sink. Place a wok over high heat. When the wok is very hot, stir the squid into the boiling water. As soon as the squid turns white, about 5 seconds, dump it into the colander and shake dry. Add the cooking oil to the hot wok. When the oil is hot, add the garlic. When the garlic just begins to brown, add the squid and the sauce. Stir and toss until the sauce glazes the squid, about 1 minute. Transfer to a platter or dinner plates and serve at once.

Clams and Mussels

Clams and mussels are easy to cook in the wok, and are such a great taste sensation that they should be a regular part of home dinners. Only buy mussels and clams that are tightly closed, which indicates that they are still alive and thus at the very peak of freshness. To store, transfer them to a colander or sieve placed in a large bowl. Cover with a kitchen towel saturated with cold water, place a few handfuls of ice cubes on top of the towel, and refrigerate. Stored in this manner, mussels and clams will breathe and stay fresh for 24 hours. One hour before stir-frying mussels, and 4 hours before stir-frying clams, place them in a bowl, cover with cold water, and give them a few vigorous stirs with your hands. Discard any that are not tightly closed, as this indicates that they are about to or already have perished. Because of this attrition, it's a good idea to buy a few extra mussels or clams just in case you have to discard some.

The stir-fry dance steps are modified when cooking mussels and clams. Mussels and clams are steamed in a covered wok until they open, and then are temporarily transferred to a colander. Once the vegetables have been stir-fried and the sauce added, the mussels or clams are plunged back into the wok for a quick glazing with the sauce.

There are four types of clams commonly sold in this country: manila, steamer, cherrystone, and littleneck. Make the extra effort and always search out a market that sells manila clams. These cook in a few minutes, pop open all at the same time, have virtually no sand hidden within, and taste marvelously tender. Steamer clams = sand = a ruined dinner. Cherrystone and littlenecks take much longer to cook than manila clams, open at an uneven rate, and have a rubbery texture.

Manila clams...
our favorite!

Clams in Hoisin Tangerine Sauce

SERVES 2 TO 4

2 pounds manila clams, all tightly closed
3 yellow zucchini
2 whole green onions
3 cloves garlic, finely minced
2 tablespoons flavorless cooking oil
Hoisin Tangerine Sauce (page 28) or your favorite wok sauce

(continued)

Advance Preparation Scrub the clams. Cut the zucchini into diamond-shaped pieces as shown on page 14. Cut the green onions on a sharp diagonal into 1-inch lengths. Combine the zucchini, onions, and garlic (no more than 4 cups total). Cover and refrigerate until 5 minutes before cooking. *Can be completed to this point up to 8 hours in advance of last-minute cooking.*

Last-Minute Cooking Review the wok cooking outline on pages 18 and 19. Place a colander inside a large bowl next to the stove. Place a wok over high heat. When the wok is very hot, add 1 cup of hot water. When the water boils, add the clams. Cover and steam until all the clams open, 2 to 3 minutes. Immediately dump the clams into the colander. Discard any clams that do not open. Return the wok to high heat and add the cooking oil. When it is hot, add the vegetable mixture and stir-fry until brightened, about 1 minute. Add the sauce and bring to a low boil. Return the clams to the wok. Toss until the clams are evenly glazed with the sauce, about 30 seconds. Transfer to a platter or dinner plates and serve at once.

Mussels in Smoked Tomato Sauce

SERVES 2 TO 4

3 cloves garlic, finely minced
2 tablespoons flavorless cooking oil
4 vine-ripe tomatoes
2 teaspoons sugar
1 tablespoon oyster sauce
2 teaspoons Asian chile sauce
2 tablespoons chopped cilantro sprigs or fresh basil
2 pounds black mussels, all tightly closed

Advance Preparation Prepare a fire in a charcoal grill or preheat a gas grill. Combine the garlic and cooking oil. Cut both ends off the tomatoes, then cut in half. Sprinkle both sides of the tomatoes with the sugar. Brush the grill rack with oil, then grill the tomatoes on both sides until charred, about 2 minutes. Remove the tomatoes, peel away and discard the skins, and chop coarsely. Combine the tomatoes with the oyster sauce, chile sauce, and cilantro. Cover and refrigerate all ingredients until 5 minutes before cooking. *Can be completed to this point up to 4 hours in advance of last-minute cooking.*

Last-Minute Cooking Within 1 hour of cooking, scrub the mussels, pulling away any seaweed caught between the shells, then refrigerate. Review the wok cooking outline on pages 18 and 19. Place a colander inside a large bowl next to the stove. Place a wok over high heat. When the wok is very hot, add ½ cup of hot water. When the water boils, add the mussels. Cover and steam until all the mussels open, 2 to 3 minutes. Immediately dump the mussels into the colander. Discard any mussels that do not open. Return the wok to high heat and add the garlic-oil mixture. When the garlic sizzles, but before it turns brown, add the tomato mixture and bring to a quick boil. Pass ¼ cup of the mussel-steaming liquid through a fine-meshed sieve. Return the mussels to the wok, along with the strained liquid. Stir and toss until the mussels are glazed with the sauce, about 30 seconds. Transfer to a platter or dinner plates and serve at once.

Mussels in Smoked Tomato Sauce

Removing the Beard from Mussels:
Pull the beard off the mussel.

Cantonese Mussels with Crunchy Snap Peas

SERVES 2 TO 4

3 whole green onions
3 cups sugar snap peas
2 tablespoons finely minced fresh ginger
40 small black mussels, all tightly closed
2 tablespoons flavorless cooking oil
Cantonese Stir-Fry Sauce (page 26) or your favorite wok sauce

Advance Preparation Cut the green onions on a sharp diagonal into 1-inch pieces. Combine the green onions, peas, and ginger (you will need 4 cups total). Cover and refrigerate until 5 minutes before cooking. *Can be completed to this point up to 8 hours in advance of last-minute cooking.*

Last-Minute Cooking Within 1 hour of cooking, scrub the mussels, pulling away any seaweed caught between the shells, then refrigerate. Review the wok cooking outline on pages 18 and 19. Place a colander inside a large bowl next to the stove. Place a wok over high heat. When the wok is very hot, add ½ cup of hot water. When the water boils, add the mussels. Cover and steam until all the mussels open, 2 to 3 minutes. Immediately dump the mussels into the colander. Discard any mussels that do not open. Return the wok to high heat and add the cooking oil. When it is hot, add the vegetable mixture and stir-fry until brightened, about 1 minute. Add the sauce and bring to a low boil. Return the mussels to the wok. Toss until the mussels are evenly glazed with the sauce, about 30 seconds. Transfer to a platter or dinner plates and serve at once.

Curried Mussels with Basil

SERVES 2 TO 4

3 cloves garlic, finely minced
1 tablespoon finely minced fresh ginger
2 tablespoons flavorless cooking oil
40 small black mussels, all tightly closed
Singapore Coconut-Herb Sauce (page 26) or your favorite wok sauce

Advance Preparation Combine the garlic, ginger, and cooking oil. *Can be completed to this point up to 8 hours in advance of last-minute cooking.*

Last-Minute Cooking Within 1 hour of cooking, scrub the mussels, pulling away any seaweed caught between the shells, then refrigerate. Review the wok cooking outline on pages 18 and 19. Place a colander inside a large bowl next to the stove. Place a wok over high heat. When the wok is very hot, add ½ cup of hot water. When the water boils, add the mussels. Cover and steam until all the mussels open, 2 to 3 minutes. Immediately dump the mussels into the colander. Discard any mussels that do not open. Return the wok to high heat and add the oil mixture. When the garlic sizzles, but before it turns brown, add the sauce. Bring the sauce to a low boil and return the mussels to the wok. Toss until the mussels are evenly glazed with the sauce, about 30 seconds. Transfer to a platter or dinner plates and serve at once.

Lobster and Crab

The wok opens entirely new vistas for cooking lobster and crab. The Chinese always prefer to chop these shellfish live, then stir-fry them with a wok sauce. For lobster, gastronomic reasons require this action. Precooked and chilled lobster meat, whether boiled or steamed, that is reheated in a wok ends up rubbery textured without a hint of its original sweetness. And you can't escape "the act" by having the fish market chop the lobster, because the raw meat deteriorates quickly. So, handle this job yourself using a Chinese cleaver, or hand the cleaver to one of your dinner guests.

Crab, on the other hand, is rarely available in this country live; it is usually sold steamed and chilled. Unlike precooked and chilled lobster meat, which toughens when stir-fried, soft, sweet, and porous crabmeat is wonderful tasting when added at the final moment of a stir-fry dish. Always purchase freshly cooked crab, never frozen, and then ask the market to crack and clean it for you.

Lobster in Ginger-Butter Sauce

SERVES 2

Ginger-Butter Sauce (page 26) or your favorite wok sauce
2 tablespoons chopped fresh mint or cilantro
2 (1½-pound) live lobsters

Advance Preparation Combine the sauce and mint. Cover and refrigerate until 5 minutes before cooking. *Can be completed to this point up to 8 hours in advance of last-minute cooking.*

Last-Minute Cooking Review the wok cooking outline on pages 18 and 19. Within 30 minutes of stir-frying, bring 3 inches of water to a vigorous boil in an 8-quart pot. Add the live lobsters and cover the pot. Cook the lobsters for 5 minutes, then remove and cool to room temperature, about 15 minutes. Split the lobsters in half and remove all the meat. (We cut precooked lobsters apart using poultry shears.) The meat should be slightly undercooked; cut it into bite-sized pieces. Within 30 minutes of precooking the lobster, place a wok over high heat. When the wok is very hot, add the sauce and bring to a low simmer. Add the lobster and stir-fry until the sauce glazes the meat and the lobster is just cooked through, 15 to 30 seconds. Transfer to a platter or dinner plates and serve at once.

Lobster in Thai Black Bean Sauce

SERVES 2 TO 4

Thai Black Bean Sauce (page 27) or your favorite wok sauce
2 tablespoons chopped fresh basil or cilantro sprigs
2 (1½-pound) live lobsters, refrigerated
2 tablespoons flavorless cooking oil
¼ pound ground pork
4 cloves garlic, finely minced
⅓ cup chopped green onions

Advance Preparation Combine the sauce and basil. Cover and refrigerate until 5 minutes before cooking. *Can be completed to this point up to 8 hours in advance of last-minute cooking.*

Last-Minute Cooking Review the wok cooking outline on pages 18 and 19. Remove the lobsters from the refrigerator and chop in half lengthwise, then cut crosswise into 2-inch pieces. Using the back of the knife blade, crack the claws. Place a wok over high heat. When the wok is very hot, add the cooking oil. Add the pork and garlic and stir-fry until the meat breaks apart into individual clumps. Add the lobster and the sauce. Bring to a boil, then cover the wok tightly. Steam, stirring occasionally, until the lobster shell turns bright red, about 5 minutes. Stir in the green onions. Transfer to a platter or dinner plates and serve at once.

Must-Have Thai Crab

SERVES 2 TO 4

½ pound fresh, cooked crabmeat
¼ head green cabbage
2 whole green onions
2 tablespoons finely minced fresh ginger
Thai Coconut Sauce (page 27) or your favorite wok sauce
2 tablespoons chopped fresh basil
2 tablespoons white sesame seeds
2 tablespoons flavorless cooking oil

(continued)

For those lobster lovers not courageous enough to chop the lobster while it is alive, you can steam the live lobster first and then cook it in a hot wok within 30 minutes. Cook this dish for just two people, and serve with rice pilaf and a spinach salad as part of a romantic evening.

Lobster in Thai Black Bean Sauce

Advance Preparation Pick through the crabmeat, removing any shells. Shred the cabbage. Thinly slice the green onions on a diagonal. Combine the cabbage, onions, and ginger (you will need 4 cups total). Combine the sauce and basil. Place the sesame seeds in a dry frying pan and toast until golden, about 2 minutes. Cover and refrigerate all ingredients except the sesame seeds until 5 minutes before cooking. *Can be completed to this point up to 8 hours in advance of last-minute cooking.*

Last-Minute Cooking Review the wok cooking outline on pages 18 and 19. Place a wok over high heat. When the wok is very hot, add the cooking oil. When the oil is hot, add the vegetable mixture. Stir and toss until the vegetables brighten, about 1 minute. Add the sauce and crab. Stir and toss until the sauce glazes the food, about 1 minute. Transfer to a platter or dinner plates, sprinkle the sesame seeds over the top, and serve at once.

Crab with Bok Choy and Egg

SERVES 2 TO 4

½ pound fresh, cooked crabmeat
4 eggs
2 teaspoons dark sesame oil
2 tablespoons finely minced fresh ginger
4 stalks large bok choy
2 tablespoons flavorless cooking oil
Essential Vegi Stir-Fry Sauce (page 27) or your favorite wok sauce

Advance Preparation Pick through the crabmeat, removing any shells. Beat the eggs well and stir in the sesame oil and ginger. Roll-cut the bok choy as shown on page 14 (you will need 4 cups total). Cover and refrigerate all ingredients until 5 minutes before cooking. *Can be completed to this point up to 8 hours in advance of last-minute cooking.*

Last-Minute Cooking Review the wok cooking outline on pages 18 and 19. Place a wok over high heat. When the wok is very hot, add 1 tablespoon of the cooking oil. When the oil is hot, add the egg mixture. Scramble the eggs, then transfer them to a plate. Return the wok to high heat and add the remaining 1 tablespoon oil. When it is hot, add the bok choy and stir-fry until the leaves turn bright green, about 1 minute. Pour in the sauce and add the crab and scrambled eggs. Stir and toss until the sauce glazes the food, about 1 minute. Transfer to a platter or dinner plates and serve at once.

Fish

Success in stir-frying fish depends on purchasing the freshest fish. If the "fresh" fish has been displayed in the case for more than 2 days, or if all that's available is vastly inferior-tasting frozen fish, choose another wok recipe in this book.

It's not necessary to marinate fish. Once the stir-fry sauce is added, the fish will pick up plenty of flavor. However, if you want a more intense taste, choose any of the marinades from page 26. You'll only need to use about 2 tablespoons of marinade per pound of fish. Don't marinate the fish for more than 15 minutes, and just prior to stir-frying, be sure to drain off any liquid that has accumulated. Otherwise the oil will splatter and the food will steam rather than sear.

Since firm-fleshed fish such as tuna, shark, and swordfish doesn't fall apart when stir-fried, it can be cooked in the wok in the same manner as shrimp. Softer fish such as halibut, salmon, and red snapper can also be stir-fried, but some of the pieces will fall apart during cooking. When stir-frying softer fish, cut it thicker, into about $1/3$-inch slices.

Spicy Catfish on Vegetable Thrones

SERVES 2 TO 4

½ pound small carrots
2 whole green onions
¼ pound button mushrooms
3 cloves garlic, finely minced
1 pound fresh catfish fillets
2 tablespoons flavorless cooking oil
Szechwan Hoisin-Honey Sauce (page 27) or your favorite wok sauce

Advance Preparation Peel and then roll-cut the carrots as shown on page 13. Diagonally cut the green onions into 1-inch lengths. Cut the mushrooms into ¼-inch slices. Combine the carrots, green onions, mushrooms, and garlic (you will need 4 cups total). Cut the catfish into tiles as shown here. Cover and refrigerate all ingredients until 5 minutes before cooking. *Can be completed to this point up to 8 hours in advance of last-minute cooking.*

Last-Minute Cooking Review the wok cooking outline on pages 18 and 19. Place a wok over high heat. When the wok is very hot, add the cooking oil. When the oil is hot, add the vegetable mixture and stir-fry until the vegetables begin to brighten, about 1 minute. Pour in the sauce and gently add the catfish. Cover the wok and steam until the catfish is cooked through, about 1 minute, stirring every 15 seconds. Transfer to a platter or dinner plates and serve at once.

Tile Cutting Fish:
Cut with the knife tilted sharply toward the fish, making thin tile-shaped pieces, then cut the pieces into 1-inch lengths.

Swordfish Southeast Asian-Style

SERVES 2 TO 4

1 pound fresh swordfish, skinned
Thai Chile-Mint-Lime Sauce (page 28) or your favorite wok sauce
2 tablespoons finely minced fresh ginger
2 tablespoons flavorless cooking oil

Advance Preparation Cut the swordfish into ¼-inch slices, then cut into 2-inch lengths. Combine the sauce and ginger. Cover and refrigerate all ingredients until 5 minutes before cooking. *Can be completed to this point up to 8 hours in advance of last-minute cooking.*

Last-Minute Cooking Review the wok cooking outline on pages 18 and 19. Place a wok over high heat. When the wok is very hot, add the cooking oil. When the oil is hot, add the swordfish and stir-fry until it just begins to turn pale, about 30 seconds. Pour in the sauce. Stir and toss until the sauce glazes the fish, about 30 seconds. Transfer to a platter or dinner plates and serve at once.

Sweet-and-Sour Lemon Halibut

SERVES 2 TO 4

1 pound fresh halibut fillet, skinned
2 zucchini
2 whole green onions
3 tablespoons finely minced fresh ginger
2 tablespoons flavorless cooking oil
Sweet-and-Sour Lemon Sauce (page 26) or your favorite wok sauce
2 cups cherry tomatoes

Advance Preparation Cut the halibut into ¼-inch slices, then cut into 2-inch lengths. Cut the zucchini into diamond pieces as shown on page 14. Cut the green onions on a sharp diagonal into 1-inch lengths. Combine the zucchini, green onions, and ginger (no more than 2 cups total). Cover and refrigerate all ingredients until 5 minutes before cooking. *Can be completed to this point up to 8 hours in advance of last-minute cooking.*

Last-Minute Cooking Review the wok cooking outline on pages 18 and 19. Place a wok over high heat. When the wok is very hot, add the cooking oil. When the oil is hot, add the vegetable mixture and stir-fry until brightened, about 30 seconds. Gently stir in the halibut and the sauce. Cover the wok and steam until the halibut is cooked through, about 1 minute, removing the lid and gently stirring and tossing every 15 seconds. During the last 30 seconds, stir in the tomatoes. Transfer to a platter or dinner plates and serve at once.

Instead of stir-frying soft-fleshed fish such as halibut and salmon, try this technique: Stir-fry the vegetables first. When they are about 1 minute from being fully cooked, gently stir in the sliced raw fish and a little sauce. Cover the wok for 15 seconds, and then stir the vegetables and fish. Repeat the covering-and-stirring process until the vegetables and fish are fully cooked, about 1 minute more. This method is described in Sweet-and-Sour Lemon Halibut, but can be used in any recipe when you want to substitute a soft-fleshed fish for a firm-fleshed one.

Swordfish Southeast Asian–Style

Cantonese Salmon with Asparagus

SERVES 2 TO 4

1 pound salmon fillet, skinned and boned
1 bunch asparagus, woody ends snapped off
4 whole green onions
2 tablespoons finely minced fresh ginger
2 tablespoons flavorless cooking oil
Cantonese Stir-Fry Sauce (page 26) or your favorite wok sauce
2 cups bean sprouts

Advance Preparation Cut the salmon into ¼-inch slices, then cut into 1½-inch lengths. Cut the asparagus into ½-inch lengths. Cut the green onions on a sharp diagonal into 1-inch lengths. Combine the green onions and ginger. Cover and refrigerate all ingredients until 5 minutes before cooking. *Can be completed to this point up to 8 hours in advance of last-minute cooking.*

Last-Minute Cooking Review the wok cooking outline on pages 18 and 19. Place a wok over high heat. When the wok is very hot, add the cooking oil. When the oil is hot, add the asparagus and green onion–ginger mixture. Stir and toss until the vegetables just begin to brighten, about 40 seconds. Stir in the salmon, pour in the sauce, and cover the wok. Every 15 seconds, remove the lid, gently stir the food, and cover again. When the salmon is cooked through, about 1 minute, stir in the bean sprouts. Transfer to a platter or dinner plates and serve at once.

Terrific Thai Tuna

SERVES 2 TO 4

1 pound fresh tuna, skinned
1 tablespoon finely minced fresh ginger
2 whole green onions, chopped
1 tablespoon white sesame seeds
2 tablespoons flavorless cooking oil
All-Purpose Thai Marinade (page 26) or your favorite wok marinade

Advance Preparation Cut the tuna into ¼-inch slices, then cut into 2-inch lengths. Combine the ginger and green onions. Place the sesame seeds in a dry frying pan and toast until golden, about 2 minutes. Cover and refrigerate all ingredients except the sesame seeds until 5 minutes before cooking. *Can be completed to this point up to 8 hours in advance of last-minute cooking.*

Last-Minute Cooking Review the wok cooking outline on pages 18 and 19. Place a wok over high heat. When the wok is very hot, add 1 tablespoon of the cooking oil. When the oil is hot, add the tuna and stir-fry until it just begins to turn pale, about 30 seconds. Transfer to a plate and return the wok to high heat. Add the remaining 1 tablespoon oil. When it is hot, add the ginger mixture and stir-fry for 15 seconds. Pour in the marinade and return the tuna to the wok. Stir and toss until the marinade glazes the food, about 30 seconds. The tuna should still be undercooked in the center. Transfer to a platter or dinner plates. Sprinkle the sesame seeds over and serve at once.

Chicken

You'll achieve great-tasting chicken stir-frys if you follow just a few simple steps. First, whenever possible buy organic chicken because it has a more intense taste and firmer texture than the bland, mushy, mass-produced birds. Second, remember the wok rule: the smaller the food is cut, the quicker it cooks and the better it tastes. Chicken cut into pieces larger than ½-inch square will toughen on the outside by the time the interior is fully cooked. Third, if you will be stir-frying and then setting the chicken aside while cooking the vegetables, some of the chicken pieces should still appear a little under-cooked on the **outside** *when they are set aside. The chicken will continue cooking as it rests, and then will finish cooking perfectly when added back to the wok with the vegetables.*

Moo Goo Gai Pan

SERVES 2 TO 4

1 pound boneless, skinless chicken breast meat
All-Purpose Chinese Marinade (page 26) or your favorite wok marinade
½ pound shiitake, chanterelle, or morel mushrooms, brushed clean
2 whole green onions
3 cloves garlic, finely minced
3 tablespoons flavorless cooking oil
Cantonese Stir-Fry Sauce (page 26) or your favorite wok sauce

Advance Preparation Cut the chicken into ½-inch cubes as shown here. Place the chicken in a bowl and add the marinade. Mix well. If using shiitake mushrooms, cut off the stems. Cut the mushrooms into ⅛-inch slices. Cut the green onions on a sharp diagonal into 1-inch lengths. Combine the mushrooms, green onions, and garlic (you will need 4 cups total). Cover and refrigerate all ingredients until 5 minutes before cooking. *Can be completed to this point up to 8 hours in advance of last-minute cooking.*

Last-Minute Cooking Review the wok cooking outline on pages 18 and 19. Place a wok over high heat. When the wok is very hot, add 1½ tablespoons of the cooking oil. When the oil is hot, add the chicken and stir and toss until it is mostly opaque, about 2 minutes. Transfer the chicken to a plate and return the wok to high heat. Add the remaining 1½ tablespoons oil. When it is hot, add the vegetable mixture and stir-fry until the mushrooms soften slightly, about 2 minutes. Pour in the sauce and return the chicken to the wok. Stir and toss until the sauce glazes the food, about 1 minute. Transfer to a platter or dinner plates and serve at once.

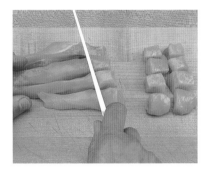

Cubing Chicken or Duck Breasts:
Cut the chicken or duck breasts lengthwise into ½-inch-wide strips. Cut across the strips to make ½-inch cubes.

Mushrooms and chicken are a classic combination in many cuisines, especially Chinese. For stir-frying, any of the firm varieties of mushroom will work. But don't select the softer textured enoki or oyster mushrooms, as they will become mushy in the wok.

Wok Chicken with Herbs

SERVES 2 TO 4

1 pound boneless, skinless chicken breast meat
All-Purpose Chinese Marinade (page 26) or your favorite wok marinade
2 tablespoons flavorless cooking oil
¼ cup cilantro sprigs, mint leaves, or small basil leaves

Advance Preparation Cut the chicken into rectangles as shown on page 70. Place the chicken in a bowl and add the marinade. Mix well, cover, and refrigerate until 5 minutes before cooking. Can be completed to this point up to 8 hours in advance of last-minute cooking.

Last-Minute Cooking Review the wok cooking outline on pages 18 and 19. Place a wok over high heat. When the wok is very hot, add the cooking oil. When the oil is hot, add the chicken and stir and toss until it is mostly opaque, about 2 minutes. Stir in the cilantro. Transfer to a platter or dinner plates and serve at once.

Roast Chicken with Eggplant, Szechwan-Style

SERVES 2 TO 4

2 ½ pounds roasted chicken
3 Japanese or Chinese eggplants
1 yellow onion
¼ cup finely minced fresh ginger
3 cloves garlic, finely minced
Szechwan Hoisin-Honey Sauce (page 27) or your favorite wok sauce
2 tablespoons chopped cilantro sprigs
3 tablespoons flavorless cooking oil

Advance Preparation Pull the chicken meat off the bone and discard the skin. Cut the meat into rectangles as shown on page 70 until you have 2 to 3 cups. Quarter the eggplants lengthwise, then cut crosswise into ¼-inch pieces. Peel and cut the onion into ½-inch cubes. Combine the eggplant, onion, ginger, and garlic (you will need 4 cups total). Combine the sauce and cilantro. Cover and refrigerate all ingredients until 5 minutes before cooking. *Can be completed to this point up to 8 hours in advance of last-minute cooking.*

Last-Minute Cooking Review the wok cooking outline on pages 18 and 19. Place a wok over high heat. When the wok is very hot, add the cooking oil. When the oil is hot, add the vegetable mixture and stir-fry for 30 seconds. Add ¼ cup water, cover the wok, and steam the vegetables for 90 seconds. Remove the lid and stir-fry for a few seconds. If the eggplant has not softened slightly, cover the wok again and repeat the steaming process. When the eggplant is cooked, pour in the sauce and add the chicken. Stir and toss until the sauce glazes the food, about 1 minute. Transfer to a platter or dinner plates and serve at once.

Wok Chicken with Herbs

Matchstick Cutting Chicken or Duck Breasts:
Cut the chicken or duck breasts in half horizontally. Cut crosswise into ⅛-inch-wide slices. Cut the slices into 1-inch lengths.

The Chinese have a surprising technique for toasting raw cashews and peanuts. The nuts are submerged in cold cooking oil, and then heated in the oil until the nuts turn golden. At this point they are immediately drained in a sieve (the oil is discarded). Once the nuts return to room temperature, there is no greasy film on the exterior, and they have a most intense nut taste—far better than if the nuts had been toasted in the oven.

Classic Cashew Chicken

SERVES 2 TO 4

1 pound boneless, skinless chicken breast meat
All-Purpose Thai Marinade (page 26) or your favorite wok marinade
1½ cups matchstick-cut carrots (page 13)
1½ cups thin asparagus, cut on the diagonal into 1-inch lengths
1 cup raw cashews
1 cup flavorless cooking oil
Essential Vegi Stir-Fry Sauce (page 27) or your favorite wok sauce

Advance Preparation Cut the chicken into very thin slices, about ⅛-inch wide. Cut the slices into 1-inch matchsticks. Place the chicken in a bowl and add the marinade. Mix well. Combine the carrots and asparagus. In a small saucepan, combine the cashews and cooking oil. Place over high heat and stir. As soon as the nuts turn light golden, drain them in a sieve placed over another saucepan to catch the oil. Allow the nuts to cool to room temperature, then set aside. Reserve 3 tablespoons of the cooking oil, and discard the remaining oil. Cover and refrigerate all ingredients except the nuts until 5 minutes before cooking. *Can be completed to this point up to 8 hours in advance of last-minute cooking.*

Last-Minute Cooking Review the wok cooking outline on pages 18 and 19. Place a wok over high heat. When the wok is very hot, add 1½ tablespoons of the reserved cooking oil. When the oil is hot, add the chicken and stir and toss until it is mostly opaque, about 90 seconds. Transfer to a plate and return the wok to high heat. Add the remaining 1½ tablespoons oil. When it is hot, add the vegetables and stir-fry until softened slightly, about 2 minutes. Pour in the sauce and return the chicken to the wok. Add the cashews and stir and toss until the sauce glazes the food, about 1 minute. Transfer to a platter or dinner plates and serve at once.

Rainbow Chicken with Thai High Sauce

SERVES 2 TO 4

1 pound boneless, skinless chicken breast meat
All-Purpose Thai Marinade (page 26) or your favorite wok marinade
1 large yellow onion
1 red bell pepper, stemmed and seeded
1 orange or yellow bell pepper, stemmed and seeded
3 tablespoons flavorless cooking oil
Thai High Sauce (page 28) or your favorite wok sauce

Advance Preparation Cut the chicken into ½-inch cubes as shown on page 65. Place the chicken in a bowl and add the marinade. Mix well. Peel and cut the onion into ½-inch cubes. Cut both peppers into ½-inch cubes. Combine the onion and peppers (you will need 4 cups total). Cover and refrigerate all ingredients until 5 minutes before cooking. *Can be completed to this point up to 8 hours in advance of last-minute cooking.*

(continued)

Classic Cashew Chicken

Last-Minute Cooking Review the wok cooking outline on pages 18 and 19. Place a wok over high heat. When the wok is very hot, add 1½ tablespoons of the cooking oil. When the oil is hot, add the chicken and stir and toss until it is mostly opaque, about 2 minutes. Transfer the chicken to a plate and return the wok to high heat. Add the remaining 1½ tablespoons oil. When it is hot, add the vegetable mixture and stir-fry until it brightens, about 1 minute. Pour in the sauce and return the chicken to the wok. Stir and toss until the sauce glazes the food, about 1 minute. Transfer to a platter or dinner plates and serve at once.

Spicy Garlic Chicken and Cauliflower

SERVES 2 TO 4

1 pound boneless, skinless chicken thigh meat
Spicy Tangerine Marinade (page 26) or your favorite wok marinade
½ head cauliflower
2 whole green onions
3 tablespoons flavorless cooking oil
Asian Garlic Sauce (page 27) or your favorite wok sauce

Advance Preparation Cut the chicken into rectangles as shown here. Place the chicken in a bowl and add the marinade. Mix well. Cut the cauliflower into small florets. Cut the green onions on a sharp diagonal into 1-inch lengths. Combine the cauliflower and green onions (you will need 4 cups total). Cover and refrigerate all ingredients until 5 minutes before cooking. *Can be completed to this point up to 8 hours in advance of last-minute cooking.*

Last-Minute Cooking Review the wok cooking outline on pages 18 and 19. Place a wok over high heat. When the wok is very hot, add 1½ tablespoons of the cooking oil. When the oil is hot, add the chicken and stir and toss until it is mostly opaque, about 2 minutes. Transfer to a plate and return the wok to high heat. Add the remaining 1½ tablespoons oil. When it is hot, add the vegetable mixture and stir-fry for 30 seconds. Add ¼ cup water, cover the wok, and steam for 30 seconds. Remove the cover, pour in the sauce, and return the chicken to the wok. Stir and toss until the sauce glazes the food, about 1 minute. Transfer to a platter or dinner plates and serve at once.

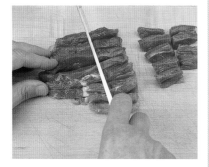

Rectangular Cutting Chicken or Duck Breasts:

Cut the chicken or duck breasts lengthwise into ¼-inch-wide slices. Place the strips together and cut across into 1-inch lengths.

Crunchy Celery Chicken with Peanut Glaze

SERVES 2 TO 4

1 pound boneless, skinless chicken breast meat
All-Purpose Chinese Marinade (page 26) or your favorite wok marinade
5 stalks celery

3 whole green onions
4 cloves garlic, finely minced
3 tablespoons flavorless cooking oil
Spicy Peanut Stir-Fry Sauce (page 27) or your favorite wok sauce

Advance Preparation Cut the chicken into rectangles as shown on page 70. Place the chicken in a bowl and add the marinade. Mix well. Roll-cut the celery as shown on page 14. Cut the green onions on a sharp diagonal into 1-inch lengths. Combine the celery, green onions, and garlic (you will need 4 cups total). Cover and refrigerate all ingredients until 5 minutes before cooking. *Can be completed to this point up to 8 hours in advance of last-minute cooking.*

Last-Minute Cooking Review the wok cooking outline on pages 18 and 19. Place a wok over high heat. When the wok is very hot, add 1½ tablespoons of the cooking oil. When the oil is hot, add the chicken and stir and toss until it is mostly opaque, about 2 minutes. Transfer the chicken to a plate and return the wok to high heat. Add the remaining 1½ tablespoons oil. When it is hot, add the vegetable mixture and stir-fry until the celery brightens, about 30 seconds. Pour in the sauce and return the chicken to the wok. Stir and toss until the sauce glazes the food, about 1 minute. Transfer to a platter or dinner plates and serve at once.

Thai Thighs with Peanuts

SERVES 2 TO 4

1 pound boneless, skinless chicken thigh meat
All-Purpose Thai Marinade (page 26) or your favorite wok marinade
5 whole green onions
3 cloves garlic, finely minced
2 tablespoons finely minced fresh ginger
3 tablespoons flavorless cooking oil
Thai Black Bean Sauce (page 27) or your favorite wok sauce
½ cup roasted peanuts, unsalted

Advance Preparation Cut the chicken into ¼-inch cubes. Place the chicken in a bowl and add the marinade. Mix well. Cut the green onions on a sharp diagonal into 1-inch lengths. Combine the onions, garlic, and ginger. Cover and refrigerate all ingredients until 5 minutes before cooking. *Can be completed to this point up to 8 hours in advance of last-minute cooking.*

Last-Minute Cooking Review the wok cooking outline on pages 18 and 19. Place a wok over high heat. When the wok is very hot, add 1½ tablespoons of the cooking oil. When the oil is hot, add the chicken and stir and toss until it is mostly opaque, about 1 minute. Transfer the chicken to a plate and return the wok to high heat. Add the remaining 1½ tablespoons oil. When it is hot, add the vegetable mixture and stir-fry until the green onions brighten, about 1 minute. Pour in the sauce and return the chicken to the wok. Add the peanuts and stir and toss until the sauce glazes the food, about 30 seconds. Transfer to a platter or dinner plates and serve at once.

Chicken thigh meat is wonderfully tender when stir-fried. Even when you purchase boned and skinned thighs from the market, it will still take some time to trim off the little pieces of fat adhering to the meat. You can use breast and thigh meat interchangeably in all chicken stir-fry recipes.

Game Birds

*I*t's hard to find a cuisine in which game birds are prepared in more varied ways than Chinese. Salt baked quail, crispy Szechwan quail, diced squab in lettuce cups, anise-scented clay pot squab, and tea-smoked squab are just a few of the listings you might find on the menu of a large Chinese restaurant.

Butchers at many gourmet supermarkets sell fresh duck breasts 1 to 2 per package, boneless, skin on, and shrink-wrapped. It's worth the effort to order these because stir-fried fresh duck is one of the great taste triumphs of the Chinese kitchen.

If you are a game bird lover, fresh quail and squab are available at many Chinatown markets. These birds are also raised commercially in many states. Ask your butcher to place a special order for you. The quail recipes included here specify "boned" quail, meaning that the breast bones have been removed, but the leg and wing bones remain intact. For wok cooking, quail and squab are cut into pieces, then browned in the wok before the stir-fry sauce is added. As the game birds cook, the sauce becomes concentrated into a fantastic tasting glaze.

Rosemary-Hoisin-Glazed Squab

SERVES 2

2 (12-ounce) squab
3 cloves garlic, finely minced
2 tablespoons flavorless cooking oil
Rosemary-Hoisin Sauce (page 28) or your favorite wok sauce

Advance Preparation Cut off the squab legs and cut them in half through the joint between the drumsticks and thighs. Cut the squab in half along the breast bone; cut away and discard the backbone. Cut each breast in half crosswise, making a total of 8 pieces. Cover and refrigerate until 5 minutes before cooking. Combine the garlic and cooking oil. *Can be completed to this point up to 8 hours in advance of last-minute cooking.*

Last-Minute Cooking Review the wok cooking outline on pages 18 and 19. Place a wok over high heat. When the wok is very hot, add the cooking oil. When oil is hot, add the squab and stir and toss until it is almost opaque, about 3 minutes. Add the sauce. Stir and toss for 1 minute, then cover the wok tightly. Decrease the heat to achieve a simmer. Every 30 seconds, remove the lid and briefly stir the squab before replacing the lid. The squab is done when the meat is pink-to-red in the interior, 3 to 4 minutes total cooking time. Transfer to a platter or dinner plates and serve at once.

Cutting Squab into Pieces

*W*hereas quail are stir-fried entirely in an open wok, the larger-sized squab are cooked by alternating stir-frying and covering the wok for 30 seconds at a time.

Chinese Roast Duck with Asparagus

SERVES 2 TO 4

1 Chinatown roast duck
1 bunch asparagus, woody ends snapped off
4 cloves garlic, finely minced
Cantonese Stir-Fry Sauce (page 26) or your favorite wok sauce
¼ cup chopped cilantro sprigs
2 tablespoons flavorless cooking oil
1½ cups bean sprouts

Advance Preparation Pull away and discard the duck skin. Remove the meat from the bones, then cut into 1 by ½ by ¼-inch rectangles. If the asparagus is thin, cut on a sharp diagonal into 1-inch lengths; if it is thick, roll-cut it as shown on page 13. Combine the asparagus and garlic (you will need 4 cups total). Combine the sauce and cilantro. Cover and refrigerate all ingredients until 5 minutes before cooking. *Can be completed to this point up to 8 hours in advance of last-minute cooking.*

Last-Minute Cooking Review the wok cooking outline on pages 18 and 19. Place a wok over high heat. When the wok is very hot, add the cooking oil. When the oil is hot, add the asparagus mixture and stir-fry until the asparagus brightens, about 90 seconds. Pour in the sauce and add the duck. Stir and toss until the sauce glazes the food, about 1 minute, then stir in the bean sprouts. Transfer to a platter or dinner plates and serve at once.

Chinese roast duck adds a fantastic taste to stir-fried vegetables. Roast duck is available at all Chinese and Vietnamese markets. Buy several, pull the meat off the carcass in large pieces, discard the skin, wrap the meat in small packages, and freeze. Now you'll have the alluring, anise-scented roast duck to perk up any work-night vegetable stir-fry.

Singapore Duck with Fresh Peas

SERVES 2

1 pound boneless duck breasts, skinned
All-Purpose Thai Marinade (page 26) or your favorite wok marinade
3 whole green onions
1 cup shelled fresh or frozen and thawed peas
2 tablespoons finely minced fresh ginger
2 cloves garlic, finely minced
3 tablespoons flavorless cooking oil
Singapore Coconut-Herb Sauce (page 26) or your favorite wok sauce
2 cups cherry tomatoes

Advance Preparation Cut the duck into ¼-inch strips, then cut into ½-inch lengths. Place the duck in a bowl and add the marinade. Mix well. Cut the green onions on a sharp diagonal into 1-inch lengths. Combine the green onions, peas, ginger, and garlic (no more than 4 cups total). Cover and refrigerate all ingredients until 5 minutes before cooking. *Can be completed to this point up to 8 hours in advance of last-minute cooking.*

Try substituting duck for any other type of meat called for in a searing hot wok. Unlike chicken pieces that must be completely cooked in the center, we prefer duck slightly undercooked so that the center of each piece has a reddish to pink hue. Cooked in this manner, the duck will taste marvelously succulent, and is completely safe to eat.

(continued)

Last-Minute Cooking Review the wok cooking outline on pages 18 and 19. Place a wok over high heat. When the wok is very hot, add 1½ tablespoons of the cooking oil. When the oil is hot, add the duck and stir and toss until it is no longer pink on the outside, about 2 minutes. Transfer to a plate and return the wok to high heat. Add the remaining 1½ tablespoons oil. When it is hot, add the vegetable mixture. If the peas are fresh, add ¼ cup water and cover the wok. When the peas turn bright green, after about 30 seconds, remove the cover. Add the sauce and tomatoes and return the duck to the wok. Stir and toss until the sauce glazes the food, about 1 minute. Transfer to a platter or dinner plates and serve at once.

Almond Duck

SERVES 2 TO 4

1 cup raw slivered almonds or whole blanched almonds
3 ears fresh white corn, husked
1 red bell pepper
4 whole green onions, chopped
1 pound boneless duck breasts, skinned
4 cloves garlic, finely minced
All-Purpose Chinese Marinade (page 26) or your favorite wok marinade
2 tablespoons flavorless cooking oil
Hoisin Tangerine Sauce (page 28) or your favorite wok sauce

Advance Preparation Preheat the oven to 325°. Spread the almonds on a baking sheet and toast until golden, about 15 minutes. Cut the kernels from the corncobs. Stem and seed the pepper and cut into ½-inch cubes. Combine the corn, red pepper, and green onions (you will need 4 cups). Cut the duck breasts into rectangles as shown on page 70. Place the duck in a bowl and add the garlic and marinade. Mix well. Cover and refrigerate all ingredients except the nuts until 5 minutes before cooking. *Can be completed to this point up to 8 hours in advance of last-minute cooking.*

Last-Minute Cooking Review the wok cooking outline on pages 18 and 19. Place a wok over high heat. When the wok is very hot, add 1 tablespoon of the cooking oil. When the oil is hot, add the duck and stir and toss until it is no longer pink on the outside, about 2 minutes. Transfer to a plate and return the wok to high heat. Add the remaining 1 tablespoon oil. When it is hot, add the vegetable mixture and stir-fry for 30 seconds, until brightened. Return the duck to the wok and add the sauce and almonds. Stir and toss until the sauce glazes the food, about 1 minute. Transfer to a platter or dinner plates and serve at once.

Almond Duck

Quail with Mint, Basil, and Pine Nuts

SERVES 2

4 fresh quail, breast bones removed
½ cup pine nuts
2 tablespoons finely minced fresh ginger
3 cloves garlic, finely minced
Really Risqué Sauce (page 27) or your favorite wok sauce
¼ cup chopped fresh mint
¼ cup chopped fresh basil
2 tablespoons flavorless cooking oil

Advance Preparation Preheat the oven to 325°. Cut the quail in half and then cut into quarters. Spread the pine nuts on a baking sheet and toast until golden, about 8 minutes. Combine the ginger and garlic. Combine the sauce, mint, and basil. Cover and refrigerate all ingredients except the pine nuts until 5 minutes before cooking. *Can be completed to this point up to 8 hours in advance of last-minute cooking.*

Last-Minute Cooking Review the wok cooking outline on pages 18 and 19. Place a wok over high heat. When the wok is very hot, add the cooking oil. When the oil is hot, add the ginger-garlic mixture and the quail. Stir and toss until the quail is almost opaque, about 2 minutes. Add the sauce. Stir and toss until the quail is just cooked through and the sauce glazes the quail, about 2 minutes. Stir in the pine nuts. Transfer to a platter or dinner plates and serve at once.

Use your favorite wok marinade or stir-fry sauce as a marinade for barbecuing, omitting any cornstarch. Marinate the poultry for 30 minutes. Then grill, brushing on any extra marinade during cooking.

Thai Seared Quail

SERVES 2

4 fresh quail, breast bones removed
2 tablespoons flavorless cooking oil
Thai High Sauce (page 28) or your favorite wok sauce

Advance Preparation Cut the quail in half and then cut into quarters. Cover and refrigerate until 5 minutes before cooking. *Can be completed to this point up to 8 hours in advance of last-minute cooking.*

Last-Minute Cooking Review the wok cooking outline on pages 18 and 19. Place a wok over high heat. When the wok is very hot, add the cooking oil. When the oil is hot, add the quail and stir and toss until it is almost opaque, about 2 minutes. Add the sauce. Stir and toss until the quail is just cooked through and the sauce glazes the pieces, about 2 minutes. Transfer to a platter or dinner plates and serve at once.

Quail with Mint, Basil, and Pine Nuts with Asparagus in Ginger-Butter Sauce (page 37)

Pork and Veal

*P*ork and veal make wonderful choices for wok cooking. Briefly cooked, the meat is marvelously tender. Pork and veal, as opposed to beef or lamb, are fine-grained meats, thus their texture is extremely pleasing. And their subtle sweet taste means that they match well with a wide range of flavors, from the spiciest Szechwan sauce to mild Cantonese creations. When choosing pork, settle for nothing less than the most tender cut—fresh pork tenderloin. Ask the butcher to trim away the white membrane, called the silverskin, that sheathes the outside of the meat. Now all you have to do is cut the meat into thin slices across the grain, marinate for a few minutes, and advance toward the hot wok! When choosing veal, tenderness is the key. Buy boned veal loin, tenderloin, or use the meat from thick veal loin chops.

Tender Thai Pork

SERVES 2 TO 4

1 pound pork tenderloin, silverskin removed
Spicy Tangerine Marinade (page 27) or your favorite wok marinade
6 stalks large bok choy
5 cloves garlic, finely minced
3 tablespoons flavorless cooking oil
Singapore Coconut-Herb Sauce (page 26) or your favorite wok sauce

Advance Preparation Cut the pork crosswise into ⅛-inch slices, then cut the slices in half. Place the pork in a bowl and add the marinade. Mix well. Roll-cut the bok choy as shown on page 14. Combine the garlic and bok choy (you will need 4 cups total). Cover and refrigerate all ingredients until 5 minutes before using. *Can be completed to this point up to 8 hours in advance of last-minute cooking.*

Last-Minute Cooking Review the wok cooking outline on pages 18 and 19. Place a wok over high heat. When the wok is very hot, add 1½ tablespoons of the cooking oil. When the oil is hot, add the pork and stir and toss until it is no longer pink on the outside, about 1 minute. Transfer to a plate and return the wok to high heat. Add the remaining 1½ tablespoons oil. When it is hot, add the vegetable mixture and stir-fry until brightened, about 1 minute. Pour in the sauce and return the pork to the wok. Stir and toss until the sauce glazes the food, about 1 minute. Transfer to a platter or dinner plates and serve at once.

Chinese Roast Pork Stir Fry

SERVES 2 TO 4

1 pound Chinese roast pork
3 bell peppers, various colors, stemmed and seeded
1 red onion
3 cloves garlic, finely minced
Cantonese Black Bean Sauce (page 27) or your favorite wok sauce
2 tablespoons chopped cilantro sprigs or fresh basil
1 tablespoon flavorless cooking oil

Advance Preparation Cut the pork crosswise into ⅛-inch slices. Cut the peppers into 1-inch cubes. Peel and chop the onion into 1-inch cubes. Combine the bell peppers, onion, and garlic (you will need 4 cups total). Combine the sauce and cilantro. Cover and refrigerate all ingredients until 5 minutes before cooking. *Can be completed to this point up to 8 hours in advance of last-minute cooking.*

Last-Minute Cooking Review the wok cooking outline on pages 18 and 19. Place a wok over high heat. When the wok is very hot, add the cooking oil. When the oil is hot, add the vegetable mixture and stir-fry until brightened, about 2 minutes. Pour in the sauce and add the roast pork. Stir and toss until the sauce glazes the food, about 1 minute. Transfer to a platter or dinner plates and serve at once.

Spicy Sweet-and-Sour Pork

SERVES 2 TO 4

1 pound pork tenderloin, silverskin removed
All-Purpose Chinese Marinade (page 26) or your favorite wok marinade
2 whole green onions
Sweet-and-Sour Lemon Sauce (page 26) or your favorite wok sauce
2 teaspoons Asian chile sauce
3 cloves garlic, finely minced
1 tablespoon finely minced fresh ginger
2 tablespoons flavorless cooking oil

Advance Preparation Cut the pork into matchstick pieces as shown on page 82. Place the pork in a bowl and add the marinade. Mix well. Cut the green onions on a diagonal into 1-inch pieces. Combine the sauce and chile sauce. Combine the garlic, ginger, and cooking oil. Cover and refrigerate all ingredients until 5 minutes before cooking. *Can be completed to this point up to 8 hours in advance of last-minute cooking.*

Last-Minute Cooking Review the wok cooking outline on pages 18 and 19. Place a wok over high heat. When the wok is very hot, add the cooking oil mixture. When the oil is hot, add the pork and stir and toss until it is no longer pink on the outside, about 1 minute. Add the green onions and stir-fry until brightened, about 30 seconds. Pour in the sauce. Stir and toss until the sauce glazes the food, about 1 minute. Transfer to a platter or dinner plates and serve at once.

The roast pork sold by all Chinese and Vietnamese markets is addictive. It's fatty, sweet-tasting, crunchy from little bits of charred meat, and difficult to stop eating in the car. Add it to any vegetable stir-fry right at the end of cooking, and it will vastly improve the taste of the dish.

Mu Shu Pork

SERVES 2 TO 4

1 pound pork tenderloin, silverskin removed
All-Purpose Thai Marinade (page 26) or your favorite wok marinade
3 cups shredded green cabbage
3 cups thinly sliced button mushrooms
2 tablespoons finely minced fresh ginger
2 cloves garlic, minced
12 (8-inch) flour tortillas
1/4 cup flavorless cooking oil
4 eggs, beaten
Essential Vegi Stir-Fry Sauce (page 27) or your favorite wok sauce
1/2 cup hoisin sauce

Advance Preparation Cut the pork into matchstick pieces as shown on page 82. Place the pork in a bowl and add the marinade. Mix well. Combine the cabbage, mushrooms, ginger, and garlic. Over a medium-heat barbecue or a stovetop gas flame, lightly char the tortillas on both sides. Stack the tortillas and wrap in aluminum foil. Cover and refrigerate all ingredients until 5 minutes before cooking. *Can be completed to this point up to 8 hours in advance of last-minute cooking.*

Last-Minute Cooking Preheat the oven to 325°. Place the tortillas, still wrapped in foil, in the oven and heat for 15 minutes. Review the wok cooking outline on pages 18 and 19. Place a wok over high heat. When the wok is very hot, add 1 tablespoon of the cooking oil. When the oil is hot, add the pork and stir and toss until it is no longer pink on the outside, about 1 minute. Transfer to a plate and return the wok to high heat. Add 1 tablespoon cooking oil. When the oil is hot, add the eggs. Scramble the eggs, then transfer them to the plate with the pork. Return the wok to high heat and add the remaining 2 tablespoons oil. When the oil is hot, add the cabbage mixture and stir-fry until brightened, about 45 seconds. Pour in the sauce and return the pork and eggs to the wok. Stir and toss until the sauce glazes the food, about 1 minute. Transfer to a platter or dinner plates and serve at once, accompanied by the hoisin sauce and hot tortillas.

Kung Pow Pork

SERVES 2 TO 4

1 pound pork tenderloin, silverskin removed
Szechwan Marinade/Sauce (page 28) or your favorite wok marinade
1 cup shelled and skinned raw peanuts
1 cup flavorless cooking oil
4 whole green onions
4 cloves garlic, finely minced
Spicy Peanut Stir-Fry Sauce (page 27) or your favorite wok sauce
1/3 cup whole dried red chiles

(continued)

Mu Shu Pork

Mu shu is one of the most famous northern Chinese dishes. Each person takes a wrapper or flour tortilla, smears the surface with a little hoisin sauce, adds the stir-fry pork, rolls the tortilla into a cylinder, and then eats with their hands. Eat quickly so that you'll be first in line for a second helping.

Kung Pow was a chef who created this dish for his employer, a famous nineteenth-century Chinese general. Classically prepared, this dish contains just chicken, peanuts, and chiles, although American Chinese restaurants tend to add all sorts of filler such as canned water chestnuts and celery! It's the dried red chiles that give this dish its pow.

Advance Preparation Cut the pork crosswise into ⅛-inch slices, then cut the slices in half. Place the pork in a bowl and add the marinade. Mix well. Combine the peanuts and oil in a small saucepan. Place over high heat and stir. As soon as the nuts turn golden, drain them in a sieve placed over another saucepan to catch the oil. Allow the nuts to cool to room temperature, then set aside. Reserve 3 tablespoons of the cooking oil, and discard the remaining oil. Cut the green onions on a sharp diagonal into ½-inch pieces. Combine the green onions and garlic. Cover and refrigerate all ingredients except the nuts until 5 minutes before cooking. *Can be completed to this point up to 8 hours in advance of last-minute cooking.*

Last-Minute Cooking Review the wok cooking outline on pages 18 and 19. Place a wok over high heat. When the wok is very hot, add 1½ tablespoons of the reserved cooking oil. When the oil is hot, add the pork and stir and toss until it is no longer pink on the outside, about 1 minute. Transfer to a plate and return the wok to high heat. Add the remaining 1½ tablespoons oil. When it is hot, add the onion-garlic mixture and stir-fry until the onions brighten, about 30 seconds. Pour in the sauce and return the pork to the wok. Add the dried chiles and stir and toss until the sauce glazes the food, about 1 minute. Transfer to a platter or heated dinner plates and serve at once.

Szechwan Pork with Charred Flour Tortillas

SERVES 2 TO 4

1 pound pork tenderloin, silverskin removed
1 small yellow onion, chopped
Szechwan Marinade/Sauce (page 28) or your favorite wok marinade
8 (6-inch) flour tortillas
2 tablespoon flavorless cooking oil

Advance Preparation Cut the pork into matchstick pieces as shown here. In a bowl, combine the pork, onion, and sauce. Mix well. Cover and refrigerate until 5 minutes before cooking. Over a medium-heat barbecue or a stovetop gas flame, lightly char the tortillas on both sides. Stack the tortillas and wrap in aluminum foil. *Can be completed to this point up to 8 hours in advance of last-minute cooking.*

Last-Minute Cooking Preheat the oven to 325°. Place the tortillas, still wrapped in foil, in the oven and heat for 15 minutes. Review the wok cooking outline on pages 18 and 19. Place a wok over high heat. When the wok is very hot, add the cooking oil. When the oil is hot, add the pork and stir and toss until it is no longer pink on the outside, 2 to 3 minutes. Transfer to a platter or dinner plates and serve at once, accompanied by the tortillas. Each person places some of the pork in a tortilla, rolls it into a cylinder, and eats with their hands.

Matchstick Cutting Pork Tenderloin:

Cut the tenderloin crosswise into thin slices. Stack or overlap the slices and cut into matchstick-shaped pieces.

Veal with Spicy Tangerine Marinade

SERVES 2 TO 4

1 pound veal loin meat
Spicy Tangerine Marinade (page 26) or your favorite wok marinade
½ cup slivered almonds
2 tablespoons flavorless cooking oil
2 cups bean sprouts
¼ cup chopped chives, about 1 bunch

Advance Preparation Preheat the oven to 325°. Cut the veal across the grain into ⅛-inch slices, then cut the slices into 1-inch lengths. Place the veal in a bowl and add the marinade. Mix well. Cover and refrigerate until 5 minutes before cooking. Spread the almonds on a baking sheet and toast until golden, about 15 minutes. *Can be completed to this point up to 8 hours in advance of last-minute cooking.*

Last-Minute Cooking Review the wok cooking outline on pages 18 and 19. Place a wok over high heat. When the wok is very hot, add the cooking oil. When the oil is hot, add the veal and stir and toss until it is no longer pink on the outside, about 90 seconds. Stir in the almonds, bean sprouts, and chives. Transfer to a platter or dinner plates and serve at once.

Tex-Mex Veal with Eggplant

SERVES 2 TO 4

1 pound veal loin meat
East-West Marinade (page 26) or your favorite wok marinade
1 yellow onion
4 small Japanese eggplants, or 1 large globe eggplant
5 cloves garlic, finely minced
3 tablespoons flavorless cooking oil
Smoky Chipotle Chile Sauce (page 28) or your favorite wok sauce

Advance Preparation Cut the veal into ¼ by ½ by 1-inch pieces. Place the veal in a bowl and add the marinade. Mix well. Peel the onion and cut into ½-inch cubes. Stem the eggplants. If using Japanese eggplants, cut in half lengthwise, then cut crosswise into ¼-inch slices. If using a globe eggplant, cut crosswise into ½-inch-wide strips, then cut into 1-inch slices. Combine the onion, eggplant, and garlic (you will need 4 cups total). Cover and refrigerate all ingredients until 5 minutes before cooking. *Can be completed to this point up to 8 hours in advance of last-minute cooking.*

(continued)

Last-Minute Cooking Review the wok cooking outline on pages 18 and 19. Place a wok over high heat. When the wok is very hot, add 1½ tablespoons of the cooking oil. When the oil is hot, add the veal and stir-fry until it is no longer pink on the outside, about 1 minute. Transfer to a plate and return the wok to high heat. Add the remaining 1½ tablespoons oil. When it is hot, add the vegetable mixture and stir and toss until the vegetables begin to sizzle in the pan, about 2 minutes. Add the sauce and immediately cover the wok. Every 30 seconds, remove the lid and stir the vegetables, then cover again with the lid. When the eggplant softens, about 3 minutes, return the veal to the wok. Stir and toss until the sauce glazes the food, about 1 minute. Transfer to a platter or dinner plates and serve at once.

Cantonese Veal with Egg, Cabbage, and Garlic

SERVES 2 TO 4

1 pound veal loin meat
All-Purpose Chinese Marinade (page 26) or your favorite wok marinade
3 eggs
1 tablespoon dark sesame oil
¼ head green cabbage, shredded
¼ cup chopped cilantro sprigs
3 cloves garlic, finely minced
¼ cup flavorless cooking oil
Really Risqué Sauce (page 27) or your favorite wok sauce

Advance Preparation Cut the veal across the grain into ⅛-inch slices, then cut the slices into 1-inch pieces. Place the veal in a bowl and add the marinade. Mix well. Beat the eggs and stir in the sesame oil. Combine the cabbage, cilantro, and garlic (you will need 4 cups total). Cover and refrigerate all ingredients until 5 minutes before cooking. *Can be completed to this point up to 8 hours in advance of last-minute cooking.*

Last-Minute Cooking Review the wok cooking outline on pages 18 and 19. Place a wok over high heat. When the wok is very hot, add 1 tablespoon of the cooking oil. When the oil is hot, add the veal and stir and toss until it is no longer pink on the outside, about 1 minute. Transfer to a plate and return the wok to high heat. Add 1 tablespoon cooking oil. When the oil is hot, add the eggs. Lightly scramble the eggs, then transfer to the plate with the veal. Return the wok to high heat and add the remaining 2 tablespoons oil. Add the vegetable mixture and stir-fry until brightened, about 1 minute. Pour in the sauce and return the veal and eggs to the wok. Stir and toss until the sauce glazes the food, about 1 minute. Transfer to a platter or dinner plates and serve at once.

Lightly scrambled eggs provide a rich taste and added moisture to many stir-fry dishes. If you are using a traditional steel wok, you'll find that the eggs will stick to the sides, so try to keep the eggs in the bottom of the wok during scrambling. Cook the eggs until firm and then transfer to a plate while you continue on with the dish. Don't bother putting a lot of effort into scraping every last bit of the egg onto the plate, since you'll be combining everything again anyway.

Cantonese Veal with Egg, Cabbage, and Garlic

Beef

*I*n Chinese restaurants, beef is often prepared by battering and deep-frying before giving it a final stir-fry with vegetables. Crunchy, slightly oily, and delicious, this technique is impossible to duplicate on our "low fire" home stoves. However, as long as you limit the amount of beef to 1 pound or less, cut it into very fine slices, and stir-fry in a very hot wok, the beef will taste tender and succulent. Exaggerate by cutting the beef thinner than you think is necessary and remove it from the wok while the interior is still pink-to-red. All of the following recipes specify flank steak, hanger steak, or beef tenderloin. These are the only three commonly sold cuts of beef that you should consider stir-frying. Although flank steak and hanger steak are more reasonably priced, they need to be cut against the grain in paper-thin slices or they will be tough. On the other hand, no matter how beef tenderloin is cut, as long as it's not overcooked, the meat will be tender.

Matchstick Cutting Flank Steak:
Cut the steak into ⅛-inch slices with the knife sharply angled. Cut the slices into matchstick-shaped pieces.

Szechwan Beef

SERVES 2 TO 4

1 pound flank steak, hanger steak, or beef tenderloin, fat and silverskin removed
Szechwan Marinade/Sauce (page 28) or your favorite wok marinade
1 yellow onion
3 tablespoons flavorless cooking oil
2 tablespoons chopped cilantro sprigs

Advance Preparation Cut the beef across the grain into ⅛-inch slices, then cut into matchstick-shaped pieces. Place the beef in a bowl and add the marinade. Mix well. Peel the onion and cut into shreds. Cover and refrigerate all ingredients until 5 minutes before cooking. *Can be completed to this point up to 8 hours in advance of last-minute cooking.*

Last-Minute Cooking Review the wok cooking outline on pages 18 and 19. Place a wok over high heat. When the wok is very hot, add 1½ tablespoons of the cooking oil. When the oil is hot, add the beef and stir and toss until it is no longer pink on the outside, about 1 minute. Transfer to a plate and return the wok to high heat. Add the remaining 1½ tablespoons oil. When it is hot, add the onion and stir-fry until it separates into individual layers, about 1 minute. Return the beef to the wok and stir and toss to evenly combine. Stir in the cilantro. Transfer to a platter or dinner plates and serve at once.

Seared Beef with Charred Tortillas

SERVES 2 TO 4

1 pound flank steak, hanger steak, or beef tenderloin, fat and silverskin removed
All-Purpose Thai Marinade (page 26) or your favorite wok marinade
5 whole green onions
8 (8-inch) flour tortillas
3 tablespoons flavorless cooking oil
Thai High Sauce (page 28) or your favorite wok sauce

Advance Preparation Cut the beef across the grain into ⅛-inch slices. Cut the slices into 1 by ½-inch rectangles as shown here. Place the beef in a bowl and add the marinade. Mix well. Cut the green onions on a sharp diagonal into 1-inch pieces. Over a medium-heat barbecue or a stovetop gas flame, lightly char the tortillas on both sides. Stack the tortillas and wrap in aluminum foil. Cover and refrigerate all ingredients until 5 minutes before cooking. *Can be competed to this point up to 8 hours in advance of last-minute cooking.*

Last-Minute Cooking Preheat the oven to 325°. Place the tortillas, still wrapped in foil, in the oven and heat for 15 minutes. Review the wok cooking outline on pages 18 and 19. Place a wok over high heat. When the wok is very hot, add 1½ tablespoons of the cooking oil. When the oil is hot, add the beef and stir and toss until it is no longer pink on the outside, about 1 minute. Transfer to a plate and return the wok to high heat. Add the remaining 1½ tablespoons oil. When it is hot, add the green onions and stir-fry until brightened, about 30 seconds. Pour in the sauce and return the beef to the wok. Stir and toss until the sauce glazes the food, about 1 minute. Transfer to a platter or dinner plates and serve at once, accompanied by the hot tortillas.

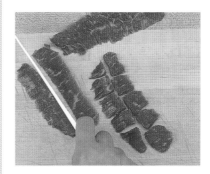

Rectangular Cutting Flank Steak:
Cut the steak into paper-thin slices, then cut the slices into rectangular or square pieces.

Glorious Beef with Mushrooms

SERVES 2 TO 4

1 pound flank steak, hanger steak, or beef tenderloin, fat and silverskin removed
All-Purpose Chinese Marinade (page 26) or your favorite wok marinade
½ pound button mushrooms or other firm mushrooms
4 cloves garlic, finely minced
3 tablespoons flavorless cooking oil
Really Risqué Sauce (page 27) or your favorite wok sauce

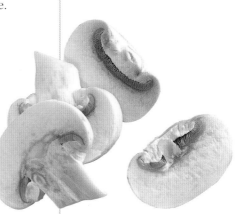

Advance Preparation Cut the beef across the grain into ¼-inch slices. Cut the slices into ½ by ½-inch pieces. Place the beef in a bowl and add the marinade. Mix well. Cut the mushrooms through the stem into quarters. Combine the mushrooms and garlic (you will need 4 cups total). Cover and refrigerate all ingredients until 5 minutes before cooking. *Can be completed to this point up to 8 hours in advance of last-minute cooking.*

Last-Minute Cooking Review the wok cooking outline on pages 18 and 19. Place a wok over high heat. When the wok is very hot, add 1½ tablespoons of the cooking oil. When the oil is hot, add the beef and stir and toss until it is no longer pink on the outside, about 1 minute. Transfer to a plate and return the wok to high heat. Add the remaining 1½ tablespoons oil. When it is hot, add the mushrooms and stir-fry until slightly softened, about 1 minute. Pour in the sauce and return the beef to the wok. Stir and toss until the sauce glazes the food, about 1 minute. Transfer to a platter or dinner plates and serve at once.

Beef Fajitas Wok-Style

For new variations, substitute beef for any of the meat recipes in this book. Or try one of our quick dinner favorites: marinate the beef for a few minutes, stir-fry it in a blazing hot wok, and then slide the beef on top of dinner salads that have been tossed in an oil and vinegar dressing. Accompanied by a glass of wine and hot dinner rolls, this makes a very satisfying work-night meal.

SERVES 2 TO 4

1 pound flank steak, hanger steak, or beef tenderloin, fat and silverskin removed
All-Purpose Chinese Marinade (page 26) or your favorite wok marinade
1 yellow onion
1 green bell pepper, stemmed and seeded
10 (8-inch) corn tortillas
3 tablespoons flavorless cooking oil
Smoky Chipotle Chile Sauce (page 28) or your favorite wok sauce
1 cup homemade or store-bought guacamole
Salsa
Lime wedges

Advance Preparation Cut the beef into $\frac{1}{8}$-inch slices, then cut the slices into very thin slivers. Place the beef in a bowl and add the marinade. Mix well. Shred the onion. Cut the bell pepper into 1 by $\frac{1}{4}$-inch matchsticks as shown on page 12. Combine the onion and bell pepper (you will need 4 cups total). Stack the tortillas and wrap in aluminum foil. Cover and refrigerate all ingredients until 5 minutes before cooking. *Can be completed to this point up to 8 hours in advance of last-minute cooking.*

Last-Minute Cooking Preheat the oven to 325°. Place the tortillas, still wrapped in foil, in the oven and heat for 15 minutes. Review the wok cooking outline on pages 18 and 19. Place a wok over high heat. When the wok is very hot, add $1\frac{1}{2}$ tablespoons of the cooking oil. When the oil is hot, add the beef and stir and toss until it is no longer pink on the outside, about 1 minute. Transfer to a plate and return the wok to high heat. Add the remaining $1\frac{1}{2}$ tablespoons oil. When it is hot, add the vegetable mixture and stir-fry until brightened, about 1 minute. Pour in the sauce and return the beef to the wok. Stir and toss until the sauce glazes the food, about 1 minute. Transfer to a platter or dinner plates and serve at once, accompanied by the guacamole, hot tortillas, salsa, and lime wedges.

Wok Magic Beef

SERVES 2 TO 4

1 pound lean ground beef
All-Purpose Chinese Marinade (page 26) or your favorite wok marinade
3 small green and/or yellow zucchini
4 cloves garlic, finely minced
3 tablespoons flavorless cooking oil
Szechwan Hoisin-Honey Sauce (page 27) or your favorite wok sauce
2 cups cherry tomatoes

(continued)

Advance Preparation Place the beef in a bowl and add the marinade. Mix well. Cut the zucchini into matchstick pieces. Combine the zucchini and garlic (you will need 3 cups total). Cover and refrigerate all ingredients until 5 minutes before cooking. *Can be completed to this point up to 8 hours in advance of last-minute cooking.*

Last-Minute Cooking Review the wok cooking outline on pages 18 and 19. Place a wok over high heat. When the wok is very hot, add 1½ tablespoons of the cooking oil. When the oil is hot, add the beef and stir and toss, pressing it against the sides of the wok with the back of the spatula. When the beef is no longer pink on the outside, about 1 minute, transfer to a plate. Return the wok to high heat and add the remaining 1½ tablespoons oil. Add the vegetable mixture and stir-fry until the zucchini brightens, about 1 minute. Add the sauce and tomatoes and return the beef to the wok. Stir and toss until the sauce glazes the food, about 1 minute. Transfer to a platter or dinner plates and serve at once.

During my college days, I was lucky enough to be included in many dinners cooked by fellow students who were Chinese. Many of the meat stir-fry dishes were made with ground beef, and the results were delicious yet inexpensive. Try substituting ground beef and ground lamb for the meat in any of the recipes in this book.

Singapore Steak with Long Beans

SERVES 2 TO 4

1 pound flank steak, hanger steak, or beef tenderloin, fat and silverskin removed
Spicy Tangerine Marinade (page 26) or your favorite wok marinade
1 pound Chinese long beans or baby green beans
2 whole green onions, chopped
4 cloves garlic, finely minced
3 tablespoons flavorless cooking oil
Singapore Coconut-Herb Sauce (page 26) or your favorite wok sauce

Advance Preparation Cut the beef across the grain into ⅛-inch slices, then cut the slices into bite-sized rectangular pieces. Place the beef in a bowl and add the marinade. Mix well. Cut off and discard the ends of the long beans. Cut the beans on a diagonal into 1½-inch pieces. Combine the beans, green onions, and garlic (you will need 4 cups total). Cover and refrigerate all ingredients until 5 minutes before cooking. *Can be completed to this point up to 8 hours in advance of last-minute cooking.*

Last-Minute Cooking Review the wok cooking outline on pages 18 and 19. Place a wok over high heat. When the wok is very hot, add 1½ tablespoons of the cooking oil. When the oil is hot, add the beef and stir and toss until it is no longer pink on the outside, about 1 minute. Transfer to a plate and return the wok to high heat. Add the remaining 1½ tablespoons oil. When it is hot, add the vegetable mixture and stir-fry for 15 seconds. Add ¼ cup water and cover the wok. Steam until the long beans brighten and are tender, about 2 minutes. Uncover the wok and add the sauce, then return the beef to the wok. Stir and toss until the sauce glazes the food, about 1 minute. Transfer to a platter or dinner plates and serve at once.

Singapore Steak with Long Beans

Lamb

S tir-fried lamb has a marvelous, rich flavor and succulent texture. Because all the fat has been trimmed away, the strong lamb taste that is so objectionable to many people is entirely absent. That's the good news. The bad news is that lamb is the most expensive kind of meat to stir-fry. Only the large end (sirloin) of the leg works for stir-frying. The shank end has too many tendons that would require laborious trimming. Lamb chops need too much trimming, and are not as tender. Racks of lamb are very expensive, and there is too much wastage. Shanks of lamb are tough, and stew meat is also tough. To speed the preparation for wok cooking, always ask the butcher to bone the leg of lamb and remove all the fat. We then spend a **little** time removing the major membranes running through the meat. Avoid overly compulsive activity! It's not necessary to remove every membrane! You'll have more than 1 pound of meat from the large end of the leg, so cut, marinate, and package the extra meat in $\frac{1}{2}$-pound amounts, then freeze it for future wok adventures. If the market requires you to purchase the whole leg of lamb, freeze the shank end and use it for curries and stews. For variations, try substituting lamb leg meat and ground lamb in any of the meat recipes in this book.

Spicy Lamb with Lettuce Cups

SERVES 2 TO 4

1 pound ground lamb
Double recipe of Szechwan Marinade/Sauce (page 28) or your favorite wok marinade
3 heads endive, or 1 head Bibb lettuce
2 tablespoons flavorless cooking oil

Advance Preparation Place the lamb in a bowl and add the marinade. Mix well. Separate the endive leaves. Cover and refrigerate all ingredients until 5 minutes before cooking. *Can be completed to this point up to 8 hours in advance of last-minute cooking.*

Last-Minute Cooking Review the wok cooking outline on pages 18 and 19. Place a wok over high heat. When the wok is very hot, add the cooking oil. When the oil is hot, add the lamb. Stir-fry, pressing the meat against the sides of the pan until the meat breaks into individual clumps and loses its pink color, about 90 seconds. Transfer to a platter. At the table, each person spoons the filling into the endive cups and eats with their hands.

G round meat requires a larger amount of marinade because its surface area is greater. So you should use 8 to 10 tablespoons of marinade for ground meat, rather than the usual 4 to 5 tablespoons. Ground meat stir-fry stuffed in lettuce cups is great served with salsa or hoisin sauce.

Spicy Lamb with Lettuce Cups

Tangerine Lamb with Onions

SERVES 2 TO 4

1 pound lamb leg meat, fat and membranes removed
All-Purpose Chinese Marinade (page 26) or your favorite wok marinade
2 large yellow onions
3 cloves garlic, finely minced
3 tablespoons flavorless cooking oil
Spicy Tangerine Sauce (page 27) or your favorite wok sauce

Advance Preparation Cut the lamb across the grain into ⅛-inch slices. Cut the slices into 1 by ½-inch rectangles. Place the lamb in a bowl and add the marinade. Mix well. Peel and shred the onions. Combine the onions and garlic (you will need 4 cups total). Cover and refrigerate all ingredients until 5 minutes before cooking *Can be completed to this point up to 8 hours in advance of last-minute cooking.*

Last-Minute Cooking Review the wok cooking outline on pages 18 and 19. Place a wok over high heat. When the wok is very hot, add 1½ tablespoons of the cooking oil. When the oil is hot, add the lamb and stir and toss until it is no longer pink on the outside, about 1 minute. Transfer to a plate and return the wok to high heat. Add the remaining 1½ tablespoons oil. When it is hot, add the onion-garlic mixture and stir-fry until the onions separate into individual segments, about 90 seconds. Pour in the sauce and return the lamb to the wok. Stir and toss until the sauce glazes the food, about 1 minute. Transfer to a platter or dinner plates and serve at once.

Spicy Lamb with Pomegranate Seeds

SERVES 2 TO 4

1 pound lamb leg meat, fat and membranes removed
All-Purpose Chinese Marinade (page 26) or your favorite wok marinade
4 cups bean sprouts
4 cloves garlic, finely minced
2 pomegranates
3 tablespoons flavorless cooking oil
Szechwan Hoisin-Honey Sauce (page 27) or your favorite wok sauce

Advance Preparation Cut the lamb across the grain into ⅛-inch slices. Cut the slices into matchstick-shaped pieces. Place the lamb in a bowl and add the marinade. Mix well. Combine the bean sprouts and garlic. Cut the pomegranates in half, submerge under cold water, and remove the seeds. Cover and refrigerate all ingredients until 5 minutes before cooking. *Can be completed to this point up to 8 hours in advance of last-minute cooking.*

Last-Minute Cooking Review the wok cooking outline on pages 18 and 19. Place a wok over high heat. When the wok is very hot, add 1½ tablespoons of the cooking oil. When the oil is hot, add the lamb and stir and toss until it is no longer pink on the outside, about 1 minute. Transfer to a plate and return the wok to high heat. Add the remaining 1½ tablespoons oil. When it is hot, add the bean sprouts and stir-fry for 30 seconds. Pour in the sauce and return the lamb to the wok. Stir and toss until the sauce glazes the food, about 30 seconds. Transfer to a platter or dinner plates, garnish with the pomegranate seeds, and serve at once.

Tofu

*T*ofu *(bean curd) means "meat without bones" in Chinese. Thus its highly nutritious character is recognized. Since it's always available in American supermarkets, bean curd is a quick way to create a healthy and tasty main course for work-night meals. You'll find bean curd labeled as "soft," "firm," and "extra firm" in markets. While soft bean curd will disintegrate in wok cooking, the other two are both good choices. We prefer firm, which has a silkier texture than extra firm.*

Because of the blandness of tofu served alone, it must be simmered for several minutes in the stir-fry sauce, so that the flavors can permeate into its center. Always choose an aggressively seasoned wok sauce, and include vegetables with a crunchy texture in order to provide contrast.

Thai Tofu with Diced Shrimp

SERVES 2 TO 4

¼ pound raw shrimp, shelled and deveined
1 pound firm bean curd
2 tablespoons flavorless cooking oil
Thai High Sauce (page 28) or your favorite wok sauce

Advance Preparation Cut the shrimp crosswise into very fine slices. Thoroughly drain the bean curd and cut into 1-inch slices. Cut the slices into 1-inch cubes. Cover and refrigerate all ingredients until 5 minutes before cooking. *Can be completed to this point up to 8 hours in advance of last-minute cooking.*

Last-Minute Cooking Review the wok cooking outline on pages 18 and 19. Place a wok over high heat. When the wok is very hot, add the cooking oil. When the oil is hot, add the bean curd and gently stir-fry for 30 seconds. Pour in the sauce. When the sauce comes to a boil, cover the wok. Every 30 seconds, gently stir the bean curd, then cover the wok again. When the sauce glazes the bean curd, about 2 minutes, remove the lid and stir in the shrimp. Continue gently stir-frying until the shrimp turns slightly pink, about 1 minute. Transfer to a platter or dinner plates and serve at once.

A little meat or seafood stirred into a dish during the final seconds of cooking adds a nice extra flavor. You might add shrimp or scallops—or we sometimes add smoked or barbecued meat from the previous night's outdoor cooking event.

Old Mrs. Ma's Tofu

Old Mrs. Ma's Tofu is based on Szechwan's most famous bean curd recipe, which was created by Mrs. Ma in the nineteenth century. It is a masterpiece of contrasting textures, the alluring flavor combinations of garlic, chiles, and herbs, and the underlying richness contributed by ground meat. The Chinese use pork, but we think ground lamb works even better.

SERVES 2 TO 4

6 cloves garlic, finely minced
¼ pound ground lamb or pork
1 pound firm bean curd
Szechwan Marinade/Sauce (page 28) or your favorite wok marinade or sauce
½ cup chicken broth
2 whole green onions, minced
⅓ cup chopped cilantro sprigs
2 tablespoons flavorless cooking oil

Advance Preparation Combine the garlic and lamb. Thoroughly drain the bean curd and cut into 1-inch slices. Cut the slices into 1-inch cubes. Combine the sauce and chicken broth. Combine the green onions and cilantro. Cover and refrigerate all ingredients until 5 minutes before cooking. *Can be completed to this point up to 8 hours in advance of last-minute cooking.*

Last-Minute Cooking Review the wok cooking outline on pages 18 and 19. Place a wok over high heat. When the wok is very hot, add the cooking oil. When the oil is hot, add the lamb and stir-fry, pressing it against the sides of the wok. Cook until the meat breaks apart into individual clumps and is no longer pink, about 90 seconds. Add the bean curd and the sauce. When the sauce comes to a boil, cover the wok. Every 30 seconds, gently stir the bean curd, then cover the wok again. When the sauce glazes the bean curd, about 2 minutes, stir in the green onions and cilantro. Transfer to a platter or dinner plates and serve at once.

Old Mrs. Ma's Tofu

Spicy Tofu

SERVES 2 TO 4

1 pound firm bean curd
2 zucchini
3 whole green onions
¼ cup raw slivered almonds
2 tablespoons flavorless cooking oil
Asian Garlic Sauce (page 27) or your favorite wok sauce
¼ cup water or chicken stock
¼ cup chopped cilantro, mint, or basil

Advance Preparation Preheat the oven to 325°. Thoroughly drain the bean curd and cut it into 1-inch slices. Cut the slices into 1-inch cubes. Cut the zucchini into 1-inch cubes as shown on page 13. Cut the green onions on a diagonal into 1-inch lengths. Combine the zucchini and green onions (you will need 4 cups total). Spread the almonds on a baking sheet and toast until golden, about 15 minutes. Cover and refrigerate all ingredients except the almonds until 5 minutes before cooking. *Can be completed to this point up to 8 hours in advance of last-minute cooking.*

Last-Minute Cooking Review the wok cooking outline on pages 18 and 19. Place a wok over high heat. When the wok is very hot, add the cooking oil. When the oil is hot, add the vegetable mixture and stir-fry until brightened, about 1 minute. Add the bean curd and toss to evenly combine. Pour in the sauce and cook for 2 minutes. If the sauce begins to cook away, add the water. Stir in the cilantro. Transfer to a platter or dinner plates and serve at once.

Tofu with Mushrooms and Asparagus

SERVES 2 TO 4

1 pound firm bean curd
2 cloves garlic, finely minced
2 tablespoons finely minced fresh ginger
½ pound button mushrooms
12 asparagus stalks, woody ends snapped off
2 tablespoons flavorless cooking oil
Cantonese Stir-Fry Sauce (page 26) or your favorite wok sauce

Advance Preparation Thoroughly drain the bean curd and cut into 1-inch slices. Cut the slices into 1-inch cubes. Combine the bean curd, garlic, and ginger. Cut the mushrooms through the stems into quarters. Roll-cut the asparagus as shown on page 13. Combine the mushrooms and asparagus (you will need 4 cups total). Cover and refrigerate all ingredients until 5 minutes before cooking. *Can be completed to this point up to 8 hours in advance of last-minute cooking.*

Last-Minute Cooking Review the wok cooking outline on pages 18 and 19. Place a wok over high heat. When the wok is very hot, add the cooking oil. When the oil is hot, add the bean curd and vegetable mixture and gently stir-fry for 30 seconds. Pour in the sauce and immediately cover the wok. Every 30 seconds, gently stir the bean curd and vegetables, then cover the wok again. When the sauce glazes the food, about 2 minutes, transfer to a platter or dinner plates and serve at once.

The best bean curd stir-fries include texture-contrasting vegetables. Play around with any of the Short-Cooking Vegetables listed on page 15.

Noodles

*S*tir-fried noodles are called "lo mein" by the Cantonese, which literally means "tossed noodles." Cold, cooked noodles are reheated in a wok along with shredded vegetables and barbecued pork or duck. This is an endlessly creative method for cooking pasta—take the following recipes as your guide. Don't get stuck on the Chinese way of only using spaghetti-type noodles. They're in a rut! Break with tradition and feel free to substitute any of the countless shapes of store-bought Italian dried pasta.

Singapore Coconut Pasta

SERVES 2 TO 4

8 ounces dried penne pasta or your favorite pasta
2 teaspoons plus 3 tablespoons flavorless cooking oil
3 to 4 green and/or yellow zucchini
2 tablespoons finely minced fresh ginger
Singapore Coconut-Herb Sauce (page 26) or your favorite wok sauce

Advance Preparation Bring 4 quarts of water to a rapid boil in a large pot. Lightly salt the water and cook the pasta according to the package instructions. When the pasta is still slightly firm, drain it, rinse with cold water, and drain again. Toss the pasta with the 2 teaspoons cooking oil. Cut the zucchini into diamond-shaped pieces as shown on page 14. Combine the zucchini and ginger (you will need 4 cups total). Cover and refrigerate all ingredients until 5 minutes before cooking. *Can be completed to this point up to 8 hours in advance of last-minute cooking.*

Last-Minute Cooking Review the wok cooking outline on pages 18 and 19. Place a wok over high heat. When the wok is very hot, add 1½ tablespoons of the cooking oil. When the oil is hot, add the zucchini and stir-fry until brightened, about 1 minute. Transfer to a plate and return the wok to high heat. Add the remaining 1½ tablespoons oil. When the oil is hot, add the pasta. Stir and toss briefly, then add the sauce. Stir and toss until pasta is heated through. Return the zucchini to the wok and stir until evenly heated, about 1 minute. Transfer to a platter or dinner plates and serve at once.

Noodles with Lamb, Chiles, and Garlic

SERVES 2 TO 4

8 ounces dried spaghetti, linguine, or your favorite pasta
2 teaspoons plus 2 tablespoons flavorless cooking oil
3 whole green onions

*A*lways cook pasta in enough water to allow the pasta to swim. Since there is no salt in dried pasta, add 2 teaspoons salt for every 4 quarts of water. The added salt brings out the full flavor of the pasta. Adding oil to the water does not prevent boiling over, nor does it keep the pasta from sticking together when left in the colander too long. To prevent overflows, just add a few tablespoons of cold water when foam starts rising in the pot. The cold water breaks the surface tension of the foam, making the foam quickly disappear. And the water is still at a furious boil.

(continued)

1 red bell pepper or large anaheim chile, stemmed and seeded
4 cloves garlic, finely minced
⅓ pound ground lamb or pork
Szechwan Hoisin-Honey Sauce (page 27) or your favorite wok sauce

Advance Preparation Bring 4 quarts of water to a rapid boil in a large pot. Lightly salt the water and cook the pasta according to the package instructions. When the pasta is still slightly firm, drain it, rinse with cold water, and drain again. Toss the pasta with the 2 teaspoons cooking oil. Mince the green onions. Mince the bell pepper. Combine the green onions, pepper, and garlic. Cover and refrigerate all ingredients until 5 minutes before cooking. *Can be completed to this point up to 8 hours in advance of last-minute cooking.*

Last-Minute Cooking Review the wok cooking outline on pages 18 and 19. Place a wok over high heat. When the wok is very hot, add the 2 tablespoons cooking oil. When the oil is hot, add the lamb and stir-fry, pressing the meat against the sides of the wok. Cook until the meat breaks into individual clumps and is no longer pink, about 1 minute. Add the pasta. Stir and toss briefly, then add the sauce and vegetable mixture. Stir and toss until pasta is piping hot, about 3 minutes. Transfer to a platter or dinner plates and serve at once.

Cantonese Wild Mushroom Pasta

SERVES 2 TO 4

8 ounces fusilli or your favorite pasta
2 teaspoons plus 3 tablespoons flavorless cooking oil
½ pound firm mushrooms such as button, shiitake, morel, or chanterelle
3 whole green onions
3 cloves garlic, finely minced
2 tablespoons finely minced fresh ginger
Cantonese Stir-Fry Sauce (page 26) or your favorite wok sauce

Advance Preparation Bring 4 quarts of water to a rapid boil in a large pot. Lightly salt the water and cook the pasta according to the package instructions. When the pasta is still slightly firm, drain it, rinse with cold water, and drain again. Toss the pasta with the 2 teaspoons cooking oil. If using shiitake mushrooms, cut off the stems. Cut the mushrooms into ⅛-inch slices. Cut the green onions on a sharp diagonal into 1-inch lengths. Combine the mushrooms, green onions, garlic, and ginger (you will need 4 cups total). Cover and refrigerate all ingredients until 5 minutes before cooking. *Can be completed to this point up to 8 hours in advance of last-minute cooking.*

Last-Minute Cooking Review the wok cooking outline on pages 18 and 19. Place a wok over high heat. When the wok is very hot, add 1½ tablespoons of the cooking oil. When the oil is hot, add the vegetable mixture and stir and toss until the mushrooms begin to wilt, about 2 minutes. Transfer to a plate and return the wok to high heat. Add the remaining 1½ tablespoons oil. When the oil is hot, add the pasta. Stir and toss for 30 seconds, then add the sauce. Stir and toss until the pasta is heated through. Return the vegetables to the wok and cook for 30 seconds more to heat evenly. Transfer to a platter or dinner plates and serve at once.

Cantonese Wild Mushroom Pasta

Thai Pasta with Chiles, Mint, Lime, and Garlic

SERVES 2 TO 4

8 ounces dried fusilli, linguine, or your favorite pasta
2 teaspoons plus 3 tablespoons flavorless cooking oil
4 cloves garlic, finely minced
4 cups sugar snap peas
Thai Chile-Mint-Lime Sauce (page 28) or your favorite wok sauce

Advance Preparation Bring 4 quarts of water to a rapid boil in a large pot. Lightly salt the water and cook the pasta according to the package instructions. When the pasta is still slightly firm, drain it, rinse with cold water, and drain again. Toss the pasta with the 2 teaspoons cooking oil. Cover and refrigerate until 5 minutes before cooking. *Can be completed to this point up to 8 hours in advance of last-minute cooking.*

Last-Minute Cooking Review the wok cooking outline on pages 18 and 19. Place a wok over high heat. When the wok is very hot, add 1½ tablespoons of the cooking oil. When the oil is hot, add the garlic and sugar snap peas and stir-fry until brightened, about 30 seconds. Transfer to a plate and return the wok to high heat. Add the remaining 1½ tablespoons oil. When the oil is hot, add the pasta. Stir and toss briefly, then add the sauce. Stir and toss until pasta is heated through. Return the sugar snap peas to the wok and cook until evenly heated, about 30 seconds. Transfer to a platter or dinner plates and serve at once.

Rainbow Pasta with Peppers and Toasted Almonds

SERVES 2 TO 4

8 ounces dried spaghetti, linguine, or your favorite pasta
2 teaspoons plus 3 tablespoons flavorless cooking oil
3 bell peppers, various colors, stemmed and seeded
3 cloves garlic, finely minced
½ cup slivered almonds
Really Risqué Sauce (page 27) or your favorite wok sauce

Advance Preparation Preheat the oven to 325°. Bring 4 quarts of water to a rapid boil in a large pot. Lightly salt the water and cook the pasta according to the package instructions. When the pasta is still slightly firm, drain it, rinse with cold water, and drain again. Toss the pasta with the 2 teaspoons cooking oil. Cut the peppers into ¼ by 1-inch matchsticks. Combine the peppers and garlic (you will need 4 cups total). Spread the almonds on a baking sheet and toast until golden, about 15 minutes. Cover and refrigerate all ingredients except the nuts until 5 minutes before cooking. *Can be completed to this point up to 8 hours in advance of last-minute cooking.*

(continued)

Thai Pasta with Chiles, Mint, Lime, and Garlic

Last-Minute Cooking Review the wok cooking outline on pages 18 and 19. Place a wok over high heat. When the wok is very hot, add 1½ tablespoons of the cooking oil. When the oil is hot, add the peppers and stir-fry until brightened, about 2 minutes. Transfer to a plate and return the wok to high heat. Add the remaining 1½ tablespoons oil. When the oil is hot, add the pasta. Stir and toss briefly, then add the sauce. Stir and toss until pasta is heated through. Return the peppers to the wok, stir in the almonds, and cook until evenly heated, about 1 minute. Transfer to a platter or dinner plates and serve at once.

Pasta with Baby Bok Choy and Peanut Essence

SERVE 2 TO 4

8 ounces dried spaghetti, linguine, or your favorite pasta
2 teaspoons plus 3 tablespoons flavorless cooking oil
5 heads baby bok choy, or 5 stalks large bok choy
¼ cup chopped cilantro sprigs or fresh basil
4 cloves garlic, finely minced
Spicy Peanut Stir-Fry Sauce (page 27) or your favorite wok sauce

Advance Preparation Bring 4 quarts of water to a rapid boil in a large pot. Lightly salt the water and cook the pasta according to the package instructions. When the pasta is still slightly firm, drain it, rinse with cold water, and drain again. Toss the pasta with the 2 teaspoons cooking oil. If using baby bok choy, cut the bottoms off. Wash and pat or spin dry. If using large bok choy, roll-cut as shown on page 14. Combine the bok choy, cilantro, and garlic (you will need 4 cups total). Cover and refrigerate all ingredients until 5 minutes before cooking. *Can be completed to this point up to 8 hours in advance of last-minute cooking.*

Last-Minute Cooking Review the wok cooking outline on pages 18 and 19. Place a wok over high heat. When the wok is very hot, add 1½ tablespoons of the cooking oil. When the oil is hot, add the vegetable mixture and stir-fry until the bok choy leaves just begin to wilt, about 45 seconds. Transfer to a plate and return the wok to high heat. Add the remaining 1½ tablespoons oil. When the oil is hot, add the pasta. Stir-fry for 30 seconds, then add the sauce. Stir and toss until pasta is heated through, about 2 minutes. Return the vegetables to the wok. Stir and toss for 30 seconds more to heat evenly. Transfer to a platter or dinner plates and serve at once.

Rice

*F*ried rice must be made from cold cooked rice. Warm or hot rice added to the wok just becomes a horrid sticky mess. The Chinese prefer white rice, always long-grain, but I love using organic short-grain brown rice. Whichever you choose, avoid converted or minute rice. These have been precooked and dried at the processing plant, and have a very poor texture.

When using long-grain white rice, rinse it thoroughly to remove the starch. Then follow the package cooking instructions. Cook the rice at least 5 hours prior to stir-frying, then chill it in the refrigerator. Before stir-frying, transfer the rice to a plastic bag and separate it into individual grains and small pieces.

One other very important point for stir-frying rice: always omit the cornstarch from your wok sauce. The sauce should not thicken around the rice grains, but should be absorbed during cooking.

Spicy Thai Fried Rice with Sausage

SERVES 2 TO 4

4 cups cold cooked white or brown rice
⅓ pound sausage links
1 red onion
¼ pound button mushrooms
3 tablespoons flavorless cooking oil
Thai High Sauce (page 28) or your favorite wok sauce, cornstarch omitted
½ cup unsalted roasted peanuts or cashews

Advance Preparation Place the rice in a plastic bag and separate into small pieces. Cut the sausage crosswise into ⅛-inch slices. Peel and chop the onion. Thinly slice the mushrooms. Combine the onion and mushrooms (you will need 4 cups total). Cover and refrigerate all ingredients until 5 minutes before cooking. *Can be completed to this point up to 8 hours in advance of last-minute cooking.*

Last-Minute Cooking Review the wok cooking outline on pages 18 and 19. Place a wok over high heat. When the wok is very hot, add 1½ tablespoons of the cooking oil. When the oil is hot, add the sausage and the vegetable mixture. Stir and toss until the sausage is no longer pink, about 2 minutes. Transfer to a plate and return the wok to high heat. Add the remaining 1½ tablespoons oil. When the oil is hot, add the rice. Stir-fry for 30 seconds, then add the sauce and return the sausage and vegetables to the wok. Stir and toss until rice is piping hot and is no longer lumpy, about 2 minutes. Add the nuts and stir to evenly combine. Transfer to a platter or dinner plates and serve at once.

*W*e like to stir-fry with the air-dried Chinese sausages available at all Chinese and Southeast Asian markets. These sausages will last indefinitely when refrigerated. You can substitute any link sausage, or even a spicy salami.

Really Risqué Fried Rice

SERVES 2 TO 4

4 cups cold cooked white or brown rice
½ cup pine nuts
1 red bell pepper, stemmed and seeded
3 whole green onions
3 tablespoons flavorless cooking oil
Really Risqué Sauce (page 27) or your favorite wok sauce, cornstarch omitted
½ cup currants

Advance Preparation Preheat the oven to 325°. Place the rice in a plastic bag and separate into small pieces. Spread the pine nuts on a baking sheet and toast until golden, about 8 minutes. Dice the bell pepper and coarsely chop the green onions. Combine the bell pepper and green onions (you will need 4 cups total). Cover and refrigerate all ingredients until 5 minutes before cooking. *Can be completed to this point up to 8 hours in advance of last-minute cooking.*

Last-Minute Cooking Review the wok cooking outline on pages 18 and 19. Place a wok over high heat. When the wok is very hot, add the cooking oil. When the oil is hot, add the rice. Stir-fry briefly, then stir in the sauce, bell pepper mixture, and currants. Stir and toss until the rice is piping hot and no longer lumpy, about 2 minutes. Stir in the pine nuts. Transfer to a platter or dinner plates and serve at once.

Fried Rice with Barbecued Pork and Eggs

SERVES 2 TO 4

4 cups cold cooked white or brown rice
¼ pound Chinese barbecued pork or ham
1 cup fresh sweet or frozen and thawed peas
2 whole green onions
2 cloves garlic, finely minced
3 tablespoons flavorless cooking oil
3 eggs, lightly beaten
Hoisin Tangerine Sauce (page 28) or your favorite wok sauce, cornstarch omitted

Advance Preparation Place the rice in a plastic bag and separate into small pieces. Dice the pork. If using fresh peas, drop them into rapidly boiling water. The moment they turn bright green, drain, transfer to ice water, then drain again and pat dry. Finely chop the green onions. Combine the peas, green onions, and garlic. Cover and refrigerate all ingredients until 5 minutes before cooking. *Can be completed to this point up to 8 hours in advance of last-minute cooking.*

Last-Minute Cooking Review the wok cooking outline on pages 18 and 19. Place a wok over high heat. When the wok is very hot, add 1½ tablespoons of the cooking oil. When the oil is hot, add the eggs and scramble until firm. Transfer the eggs to a plate and return the wok to high heat. Add the remaining 1½ tablespoons oil. When the oil is hot, add the rice. Stir-fry briefly, then stir in the sauce, pork, and vegetable mixture. Stir and toss until the rice is piping hot and no longer lumpy, about 2 minutes. Return the scrambled eggs to the wok and stir-fry until evenly combined. Transfer to a platter or dinner plates and serve at once.

Fried Rice with Barbecued Pork and Eggs with Baby Bok Choy in Spicy Garlic Sauce (page 35)

Acknowledgments

Many friends helped bring this book into print and we are deeply appreciative for your support and many contributions. Thank you Ten Speed Press, particularly Phil Wood; our publisher, Kirsty Melville; and Jo Ann Deck and Dennis Hayes in special sales. Many thanks also to our editor Holly Taines White, who did a wonderful job molding the book into its final form. Our friend and book designer, Beverly Wilson, contributed her unique vision and added so much to our pleasure working on this book. Julie Smith was the food stylist, and added her culinary and artistic skills to the photography. Thank you also to Sur La Table and the Campus Store at the Culinary Institute of America in St. Helena for lending us woks and props. Thank you all—it was wonderful to work with you on this exciting book.

Artist Credits

We want to thank the many talented artists who made the tabletop wares that perfectly accent the recipes in the photographs. It is so much fun to highlight the work of old friends and new. Ceramicist Julie Cline of Oakland, California, shows her new hand-painted work on the bowls on page 1 and the settings on pages 48, 85, 93, 100, and 103. Many thanks, Julie. Textile artist Elizabeth Haba of Oakland, California, wove the delicate mats shown on pages 51, 89, and 93. Kathy Erteman of New York City created the graphic, black and white, incised ceramic pieces on the front cover and pages 26, 27, 28, and 55.

Versatile ceramic artist Julie Sanders of the Cyclamen Collection in Oakland, California, made the colorful dishware shown on pages 34, 43, 81, and 89. Glassblower Stephen Smyers of Smyers Glass in Benecia, California, made the unique glassware on pages 40, 58, 67, and 107. Paul Hathcoat of Hathcoat Studios in Colorado Springs, Colorado, made the slumped glass dishes on pages 40 and 67. The elegant glassware on page 45 is from Nourot Glass Studio in Benecia, California.

The Thia Contemporary Craft Gallery in Berkeley, California, was the source for many beautiful pieces including the Goyer Bonneau porcelain ware on page 31, the O'Dell glasses and "All U Can Handle" fork on page 76, and the O'Dell "roly-poly" glass pieces on page 91. Thia Gallery also provided Mathew Yanchuk's ceramics on page 97. ZIA Houseworks in Berkeley, California, provided the colorful Luna Garcia dishware on pages 63, 76, and 91. The Valley Exchange in St. Helena, California, was the source for many of the hand-painted wood sculptures including those on pages 5, 96, and 109.

Thank you all for being part of *Wok Fast!* Your sense of style adds so much to the book!

Conversion Charts

Liquid Measurements

Cups and Spoons	Fluid Ounces	Approximate Metric Term	Approximate Centiliters	Actual Milliliters
1 tsp	⅙ oz	*	½ cL	5 mL
1 Tb	½ oz	*	1½ cL	15 mL
¼ c	2 oz	½ dL	6 cL	59 mL
⅓ c	2⅔ oz	¾ dL	8 cL	79 mL
½ c	4 oz	1 dL	12 cL	119 mL
⅔ c	5⅓ oz	1½ dL	15 cL	157 mL
¾ c	6 oz	1¾ dL	18 cL	178 mL
1 c	8 oz	¼ L	24 cL	237 mL
1¼ c	10 oz	3 dL	30 cL	296 mL
1⅓ c	10⅔ oz	3¼ dL	33 cL	325 mL
1½ c	12 oz	3½ dL	35 cL	355 mL
1⅔ c	13⅓ oz	3¾ dL	39 cL	385 mL
1¾ c	14 oz	4 dL	41 cL	414 mL
2 c; 1 pt	16 oz	½ L	47 cL	473 mL
2½ c	20 oz	6 dL	60 cL	592 mL
3 c	24 oz	¾ L	70 cL	710 mL
3½ c	28 oz	⅘ L	83 cL	829 mL
4 c	32 oz	1 L	95 cL	946 mL
5 c	40 oz	1¼ L	113 cL	1134 mL
6 c	48 oz	1½ L	142 cL	1420 mL
8 c	64 oz	2 L	190 cL	1893 mL
10 c	80 oz	2½ L	235 cL	2366 mL
12 c	96 oz	2¾ L	284 cL	2839 mL
4 qt	128 oz	3¾ L	375 cL	3785 mL
5 qt	160 oz			
6 qt	192 oz			
8 qt	256 oz			

* Metric equivalent too small for home measure.

Other Conversions

Ounces to milliliters: multiply ounces by 29.57

Quarts to liters: multiply quarts by 0.95

Milliliters to ounces: multiply milliliters by 0.034

Liters to quarts: multiply liters by 1.057

Ounces to grams: multiply ounces by 28.3

Grams to ounces: multiply grams by .0353

Pounds to grams: multiply pounds by 453.59

Pounds to kilograms: multiply pounds by 0.45

Cups to liters: multiply cups by 0.24

Length

⅛ in = 3 mm

¼ in = 6 mm

⅓ in = 1 cm

½ in = 1.5 cm

¾ in = 2 cm

1 in = 2.5 cm

1½ in = 4 cm

2 in = 5 cm

2½ in = 6 cm

4 in = 10 cm

8 in = 20 cm

10 in = 25 cm

Temperatures

275°F = 140°C

300°F = 150°C

325°F = 170°C

350°F = 180°C

375°F = 190°C

400°F = 200°C

425°F = 215°C

450°F = 230°C

475°F = 240°C

500°F = 250°C

Index

Other Cookbooks by Hugh Carpenter & Teri Sandison

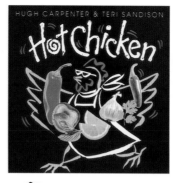

*F*ifty bold and sophisticated yet easy stir-fry recipes seasoned with a host of exciting ingredients. Perfect ideas for fresh, healthy weeknight meals or weekend entertaining. Includes more than fifty vibrant color photos.

*F*ifty wild and zesty recipes that combine chicken with the distinct flavors and cuisines of the world. Discover delicious and elegant ways to serve one of the most versatile and healthful meats. More than fifty color photos provide dramatic presentation ideas.

*F*ifty sizzling recipes for classic barbecue favorites and innovative pleasers from around the world. From simple any-night delights to elaborate weekend feasts, this tantalizing offering will heat up backyards and kitchens alike.

*F*ifty fresh and sensational recipes take pasta to new and dazzling heights. Packed with easy, inventive ideas, this is the complete resource for busy cooks at all levels of experience. Includes more than fifty exciting color photos.

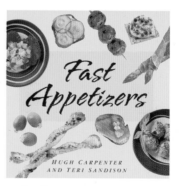

*M*ore of the winning Hot formula: sixty-plus original recipes, organized alphabetically from artichokes to zucchini, introduce a palate-tingling world of veggie-based soups, salads, pastas, sides, and entrées.

*P*latters of tender, juicy ribs have long reigned as home-cooking favorites. *The Great Ribs Book* brings you the lowdown on the different types of ribs, cooking techniques, sauces, and more. Includes more than sixty recipes pairing ribs with delectable flavors from all over the world.

*M*ore than 100 recipes, from spring rolls to pizza to caviar, that can be made in a flash, most in under 15 minutes. Whether you're hosting a cocktail party or an intimate dinner, these dishes deliver maximum flavor in minimum time.